The Two Goldsmiths. (c. 1914). Oil on wood, 28 x 20".
Collection Mr. and Mrs. Thomas M. Futter, Westfield, Massachusetts

Emil Nolde

BY PETER SELZ

THE MUSEUM OF MODERN ART, NEW YORK

IN COLLABORATION WITH THE SAN FRANCISCO MUSEUM OF ART

AND THE PASADENA ART MUSEUM

DISTRIBUTED BY DOUBLEDAY & CO., INC., GARDEN CITY, NEW YORK

LENDERS TO THE EXHIBITION

Larry Aldrich; Mr. and Mrs. David Bakalar; Dr. Walther Berndorff; Henry B. Blunden; Mr. and Mrs. Harry Lynde Bradley; Mr. and Mrs. Joseph M. Edinburg; Mr. and Mrs. Thomas M. Futter; Alfred and Anne Hentzen; Ernst Henke; Mr. and Mrs. E. Powis Jones; Andreas Kohlschütter-Fehr; Dr. Ing. Max Lütze; Mr. and Mrs. Morton D. May; Herbert Mayer; Mrs. Gertrud A. Mellon; Mrs. Bliss Parkinson; Mr. and Mrs. Hans Popper; Dr. Rauert; Mr. and Mrs. Leo M. Rogers; Dr. Henry M. Roland; Otto Schäfer; C. G. Schiefler; Mrs. Heinz Schultz; Dr. Bernhard Sprengel; Dr. and Mrs. Max M. Stern; Mrs. Ala Story; Mr. and Mrs. Eugene Victor Thaw; Dr. G. Thiem; Mr. and Mrs. William D. Vogel; Mr. and Mrs. Max Wilk; Mr. and Mrs. Donald Winston; Mr. and Mrs. C. Bagley Wright, Sr.

Busch-Reisinger Museum, Harvard University, Cambridge, Massachusetts; Wallraf-Richartz-Museum, Cologne; The Royal Museum of Fine Arts, Copenhagen; The Detroit Institute of Arts; Museum Folkwang, Essen; Kunsthalle, Hamburg; Städtische Galerie im Landesmuseum Hanover; Nelson Gallery of Art Atkins Museum, Kansas City, Mo.; Los Angeles County Museum of Art; The Minneapolis Institute of Arts; The Museum of Modern Art, New York; City Art Museum of St. Louis; Stiftung Seebüll Ada und Emil Nolde; Staatsgalerie Stuttgart.

Galerie Hoffmann, Hamburg; World House Galleries, New York.

EXHIBITIONS

The Museum of Modern Art, New York: *March 4, 1963*

San Francisco Museum of Art: *May 28, 1963*

The Pasadena Art Museum: *July 27, 1963*

Published by The Museum of Modern Art
11 West 53 Street, New York 19, N. Y.

All rights reserved

Library of Congress Catalogue Card No. 63–12115

Designed by Mary Ahern

Printed in West Germany by Christian Wolff, Flensburg

CONTENTS

ACKNOWLEDGMENT

I wish to express my thanks, above all, to the late Joachim von Lepel, who placed at my disposal the exhaustive documentary resources of the Stiftung Seebüll Ada und Emil Nolde and provided much valuable information which has been of great help to me. It is a great tragedy that Mr. von Lepel died suddenly in Venice in the summer of 1962, where he had gone to participate in the ceremonies for previous prizewinners at the Biennale. I deeply regret that he will see neither the first American Nolde retrospective exhibition nor this monograph, published in connection with it, which he was so instrumental in aiding. His widow, Mrs. Veronica von Lepel, was also most helpful to me, as was Dr. Martin Urban, the newly appointed director of the Nolde Foundation who is carrying on so competently at Seebüll and who has seen the work on this exhibition to completion.

On behalf of the Board of Trustees of The Museum of Modern Art, the San Francisco Museum of Art and The Pasadena Art Museum, I wish to express my gratitude to the Government of the German Federal Republic for its sponsorship of the exhibition and its grant to cover the costs of transportation and insurance of all German loans. We want particularly to thank three members of the German Government who have been most helpful: Dr. Dieter Sattler, head of the Cultural Department of the German Foreign Office, Dr. Hanns-Erich Haack, Cultural Counselor of the German Embassy in Washington, and Miss Haide Russell, Consul for Cultural Affairs of the German Consulate in New York.

We are grateful to the museums, private collectors and dealers who have generously made works available for the exhibition and whose names are listed on page 4. William S. Lieberman was kind enough to help in selecting the prints in the exhibition.

Neither exhibition nor book could have materialized without the help of many of my colleagues in German and Danish museums. Above all, I should like to thank Dr. Alfred Hentzen of the Hamburger Kunsthalle for his many useful suggestions and for using his good offices in expediting the shipment of paintings from Germany to the United States. I also want to acknowledge the help of Dr. Kurt Martin, Munich; Dr. Christel Mosel, Hanover; Dr. Gert von der Osten, Cologne; Dr. Werner Schmalenbach, Hanover; Dr. Günther Thiem, Hanover; Dr. Paul Vogt, Essen; and I want to thank Dr. Bernhard Sprengel, Hanover, for his cooperation. I obtained important information about Nolde and his work from Mrs. Hans Fehr, Bern; Dr. Carl Gustav Schiefler, Hamburg and Mrs. Ala Story, Santa Barbara. Werner Haftmann's previous studies of Nolde have been very useful to me. My friend, George Rickey, went out of his way during a trip to Germany in the fall of 1962 to assist us in many important details when help was urgently needed.

For special assistance in connection with the book, gratitude is due to Mr. and Mrs. Joseph M. Edinburg, Mr. and Mrs. Morton D. May, and Mrs. Gertrud A.

Mellon. The manuscript was edited by Helen M. Franc and the book was designed by Mary Ahern and seen through the press by Françoise Boas. The bibliography was compiled by Inga Forslund and the index was prepared by Lucy Lippard. Therese Varveris has been responsible for the cataloguing of the exhibition and for all the details of correspondence in connection with both book and exhibition.

Peter Selz
Director of the Exhibition

FOREWORD

Born in 1867, Emil Nolde was the exact contemporary of Pierre Bonnard. Since he grew up on the periphery of the art world, he matured considerably later than his French contemporary; but like Bonnard, he became one of the pioneers of modern art. On the foundation of impressionism Nolde developed a symbolic language of tumultuous color which serves as the primary element in a newly structured picture space through which Nolde's figures move with eruptive anxiety. A pioneer in the early years of the century, Nolde — like Bonnard — did not continue his innovations after the advent of non-objective art and cubism, when leadership went to the more adventurous Kandinsky, born one year earlier, and to the much younger Picasso (born 1881).

Nolde adhered to the ground he had conquered during the pre-war period but constantly refined his position. The oldest of the German expressionists, his derivations reach back to the ancient phantoms of Northern myth, and his concerns reach out to the primitive arts of all cultures. His painting reflects the very rhythms of Northern existence, transformed by his unique sensitivity and the esthetic revolution of his own time.

Although primarily a colorist, he became one of the few truly great graphic artists of the twentieth century. Because he was a colorist above all, he endowed watercolor with new life and vitality and a sheer visual beauty which places him in the top rank of modern artists. In this medium, he relied on improvisation and expressive spontaneity, capturing his subject matter almost by accident in a manner suggestive of later more abstract painters.

Nolde gave rise to no school and had few direct followers, but his work became of central concern to a later generation of painters, those who might be called his grandsons. It is with this relevance in mind that the first major retrospective of Nolde's work in the United States is presented a half-century after some of his most important contributions.

P. S.   January 1963

As one drives along the German-Danish border westward from Flensburg the country becomes increasingly flat. The sparse forests of the Baltic coast thin out into a few isolated clumps of trees, the nearly bald plain is relieved only by an occasional windmill or red brick church steeple and the low mounds raised centuries ago by the Dutch as foundations for farms and houses. Dikes protect the low green marshland from the North Sea, and sturdy cattle and horses roam somberly over wind-swept pastures. The immense vault of the sky is rarely clear but billows with heavy clouds. At evening the sky is richly colored by the sun as it breaks through for a little while. Then at sunset the most unexpected hues and formations appear in the skies: storms build the clouds into towering thunder-heads; when the light changes and wind sweeps across them, new configurations emerge, totally altering the mood of the land. At certain times of the year fogs blanket the plain, sometimes briefly summoning weird forms which appear and disappear in the mist, and dulling the whole countryside for long months, letting in only an occasional burst of sunlight.

The house of Seebüll in North Schleswig, where Nolde lived and worked during the last thirty years of his life, is close to the little town of Nolde where —christened as Emil Hansen—he was born in 1867. During his entire life he always returned to the marshes on the edge of the sea — indeed no modern painter was so intimately rooted to the earth and his homeland.

Taciturn and morose by nature, and highly introverted, Nolde felt most at home among the peasants of his native soil. He shared a great many of their fears, superstitions and prejudices, but with his unique artistic gifts he was able to lend these notions a mystical and often demonic aspect. He visualized himself as a mis-sionary whose privileged duty it was to create a vital, intense art of the North. Standing somewhat apart from the main stream of the art of his time, he remained essentially a regionalist, but a regionalist of genius.

In his several autobiographical volumes and in his published and unpublished letters, Nolde appears as a misanthrope: one who suffered greatly from perpetual loneliness, who was constantly aware of his inability to take part in the normal human community, yet who longed desperately for signs of friendship or at least of acceptance. From early adolescence he shunned other people; he seems frequently to have experienced deep religious feelings and mystic identifications with Christ's Passion. His attitude of melancholy mysticism remained with him throughout his long lifetime.

Nolde's copious writings are clumsy in syntax and phrased in a naïve vocab-ulary, which is only partly due to his own strange language, characteristic of the European border peasantry that is never fully at home in the culture of any lan-guage. His persistent anti-intellectualism of course merely contributed to this awkwardness of expression. Here was an artist who tells us that during his entire life he managed to read only a single book all the way through: the rather simple *Ekkehard* by Victor von Scheffel. While he waited for many years to "become an artist," he remained almost entirely self-taught. He could no more submit to a teacher than he could assimilate from the arts of past or present. After looking forward with greatest anticipation to studying in Paris and Italy, he returned, writing: "Paris has given me very little, and I had expected so much." [1] And later: "Artistically the country [Italy] gave me nothing. In no previous years had I accomplished so little and such poor work." [2]

His admiration for the primitive and the primeval was to lead him as far as the South Seas, but it was the same attitude that made him return to his native soil. A suspicion of the "isms" of the twentieth century as well as his morose personality made him rely deeply on animistic fantasy and his intense experience of nature in the forms of the sea, clouds, marshes and flowers. But in the true fashion of the romantic and the expressionist, he imposed his special artist's personality on the world, distorting its image to express his own unresolved conflicts.

It was at the age of thirty that Nolde, whose name was still Hansen, painted his first canvas, *The Mountain Giants*. Although surrounded solely by peasants in his childhood, his propensity for art had manifested itself early. While still a small child he modeled a series of clay figures which were almost at once demolished by his comrades. Soon he began coloring the pictures in his Bible, drew avidly, loved his drawing classes in school and then made attempts at painting, using the juice of elderberries and red beets. He read with admiration about Dürer and, coming across the obituary of Hans Makart, noted that an artist could still enjoy glory in his own time. While he worked on the family farm, he stole time to draw and paint, leaving the cattle hungry.

At seventeen he left the farm, took the still unusual step to the city and became an apprentice wood carver in a furniture factory in Flensburg. There he drew and carved ornaments for twelve hours a day, six days a week. Sundays he studied drawing with a professional painter. In his spare time he sketched landscapes and portraits. His determination and constancy of purpose were certainly those of a young man convinced of a mission.

After four years of apprenticeship, Nolde began his period as a journeyman cabinet maker, working briefly in a furniture factory in Munich and then in Karlsruhe, where he was able to quit his job for a short time to attend all-day classes at the School for Arts and Crafts. By 1890 his solitary wanderings took him to Berlin, but it was so difficult for him to find employment there that the further burden of bitter poverty was added to his loneliness. He sketched, did odd jobs and finally found a decent position with a large furniture manufacturer. Soon thereafter, however, he learned of a vacancy at the Museum of Industrial Arts in St. Gall and was accepted as a teacher of drawing. He was to remain there from 1892 till 1898, leading for the first time a more regulated existence. In Switzerland he sought close physical contact with nature, even daring some very perilous ascents on the Jungfrau, Monte Rosa and the Matterhorn. It was during his stay in Switzerland that he learned for the first time something about contemporary thought, from friends who talked to him of the philosophy of Nietzsche, the poetry of Verlaine and Rimbaud, the music of Wagner, the plays of Ibsen and Strindberg, the novels of Hamsun and Gorky. He went to Milan where in Santa Maria delle Grazie he saw Leonardo's *Last Supper* which made a lasting impression on him. But in the art museum in Vienna he was still not ready to pause in front of the paintings, fearing that their attraction would precipitate him too rapidly into the career of an artist. Among contemporaries he admired Böcklin and was partial to Hodler, and one day he even met a famous artist when Lovis Corinth visited St. Gall.

During this period Nolde sketched the Swiss towns and mountains, but he was especially fascinated by the peasant types and made caricatures of their faces. He did a series of grotesque and demonic masks and endowed the mountains with troll-like features in accordance with the concepts of popular fantasy and nomenclature. He made small postcards of these personified mountains and, encouraged by their reproduction in the famous magazine *Jugend,* printed an edition of 100,000 cards. Their crude and simple anti-art quality, which made no demands on intellect or esthetic sensibility, so captured popular taste that the edition was exhausted in ten days, earning Nolde 25,000 Swiss francs. As soon as he could, he gave up his teaching job and left for Munich to become a full-time student of painting. He was now thirty-one years old.

At once he applied to the famous Franz von Stuck for admission to his classes at the Academy, only to be rejected. He commented later: "How beautiful it might have been to meet there Kandinsky, Klee and perhaps also Marc, who were all students of Stuck's at that time" [3] — indeed a fascinating speculation. Instead, he studied privately with Friedrich Fehr in Munich and Adolf Hölzel in Dachau. Hölzel, who later became a pioneer of abstract painting, at that time still practiced the dark, moody naturalism which was as characteristic of the regional nature painters in both Worpswede and Dachau as it had been of the earlier Barbizon painters. Nolde at last had time to study the work of other artists; he began making structural sketches of paintings by artists who then enjoyed popularity — Böcklin, Constable, Goya, Liebermann, Menzel, Millet, Stuck, Watts, Whistler, Zorn — reducing their compositions to two-dimensional planes and paying particular attention to the contrast and balance of tonal values. The two painters whom he considered the "most significant of our time" were G. B. Watts and Arnold Böcklin, with Millet and Whistler following as close seconds. [4] He was already convinced, at least in theory if not necessarily in his choice of artists, that a great work of art had to be a fusion of "ability, fantasy and poetic power." [5]

In the autumn of 1899 Nolde went to Paris, where his great expectations were to be so disappointed. He enrolled briefly at the Académie Julian under Lefebvre and Fleuri, but found his time more profitably spent in the museums, where he made a faithful copy of Titian's *Allegory of Alfonso d'Avalos* and admired Rembrandt's *Supper at Emmaus.* He was greatly interested in Daumier's paintings

The Matterhorn Smiles. (1894). Color postcard, 5⁷/₈ x 4¹/₈″. Nolde Foundation, Seebüll

and in Rodin's sculpture which he saw at the World's Fair of 1900; he familiarized himself with impressionism, loving Manet's "light beauty" and disdaining the "sweetness of the paintings by Renoir, Monet, Pissarro, which did not appeal to my harsher Northern senses." [6] A year later, the restless Nolde moved to Copenhagen where he went through an anguished crisis in both his solitary life and his still incipient art. His loneliness at least was ended by his marriage in 1902 to a Danish girl, Ada Vilstrup. The young couple moved back and forth between Berlin, Flensburg and a little fisherman's shack on the island of Alsen, and as nobody would buy Nolde's paintings they lived in abject poverty for a good many years. Ada, who had had some theatrical training, made an unsuccessful attempt as a music-hall entertainer in Berlin, which was followed by complete physical exhaustion and a recuperative trip to Sicily during the winter of 1904-05.

At the time of his marriage the painter had changed his name from Emil Hansen to Emil Nolde — after his native village — not only because of the great number of Hansens in that part of the world, but also in order to mark the separation between his life of preparation for art and his life as an artist. During the first

Moonlit Night. (1903). Oil on canvas, 25 1/2 x 32 5/8".
Wallraf-Richartz-Museum, Cologne

Harvest Day. (1904). Oil on canvas, 28³/₄ x 35⁷/₈".
Collection Andreas Kohlschütter-Fehr, Cambridge, Mass.

Spring Indoors. 1904. Oil on canvas, 34⁷/₈ x 28⁷/₈".
Nolde Foundation, Seebüll

years of the century his work was still quite eclectic. One of his first canvases, *Before Sunrise* (page 61), borrows from Böcklin's fantasy, with two birdlike dragons on high mountain cliffs over a Leonardesque landscape. *Moonlit Night* of 1903 is painted in veiled grey tonal values related to Hölzel's paintings of Dachau moors in Bavaria, although the more Northern painter emphasizes in a quite personal way the vastness of the flat marshland lying in the mysterious moonlight, and the solitariness of the single habitation. A year later the lovely *Spring Indoors* clearly indicates his familiarity with impressionism. The composition of related warm colors, the room penetrated by light, and the quiet intimacy of the interior scene with Ada reading at a table are all very similar to the work of Bonnard. Yet, although Bonnard was Nolde's exact contemporary, the two painters never knew each other and probably never saw one another's work. Both great colorists, their paintings, except for this single example, are completely different.

Nolde was soon to go in a very different direction. He had studied the work of the impressionists and greatly respected the paintings of van Gogh, Gauguin, and Munch. However, his opinion of the German impressionists, who were the leading figures at home, was never very high. He felt they were weak imitators at a time when it was necessary to forge ahead. He wrote about the magic power pure brilliant color had for him, and in the summer of 1904 he excitedly applied the brightest pigments with a broad and vehement brushstroke to his canvas *Harvest Day*. In this canvas, the rhythms of the brushstroke and the personal feeling for the free expression of color, no longer tied directly to the object, establish him as an artist with a different approach. In a letter to his close friend Hans Fehr he relates: "I was as if intoxicated when I painted this picture. I surprised myself and was astonished by its effect, its movement and brightness." [7] Almost at once Nolde had both mastered impressionism and transformed it into a more passionate and energetic statement of great intensity.

Harvest Day was painted before he left on his Italian trip of 1904-05. Upon his return he found that it had been accepted for the important annual exhibition of the Berlin Secession. He met Carl Ernst Osthaus, one of the first patrons of advanced art in Germany, studied Osthaus' superb collection, which later became the Folkwang Museum, [8] and even sold his *Spring Indoors* to the collector. Soon he met the print connoisseur, Gustav Schiefler, who was to purchase a number of his etchings. While most of the criticism of his work was hostile and negative, at least he was now recognized. And encounters with two older painters whom he esteemed highly, Christian Rohlfs and Edvard Munch, for the first time gave him much-needed moral support for his way of painting.

Having supposed himself to be completely alone in his search for new artistic expression, Nolde was overjoyed when in February of 1906 he received a letter from Karl Schmidt-Rottluff, inviting him to become a member of the recently formed Dresden artists' group *Die Brücke* (The Bridge), which had as one of its aspirations: "to draw to itself all revolutionary and fermenting elements." [9] The young *Brücke* artists, seeing a few paintings Nolde had exhibited at the Galerie Ernst Arnold in Dresden, admired his "tempests of color" and expressed their esteem in this invitation. Nolde speaks of his amazement and joy at recognition by his peers: "I was not alone! There were other young painters imbued with the future, with aims similar to my own." [10] Schmidt-Rottluff accepted Nolde's invitation to visit him in Alsen during the early fall, at which time views and opinions were freely exchanged. In 1907 the Noldes went to Dresden, where the always sickly Ada underwent special medical treatments while Nolde enjoyed the stimulating company of the young Kirchner, Heckel and Pechstein. He was grateful to belong to a group of avant-garde artists, not only to share their ideas but also, quite practically, to join the fight for the acceptance of a new, still unnamed kind of painting, and to get his work exhibited and perhaps bought. He gladly participated in the group shows of *Die Brücke* not only in Dresden, but also in Hamburg, Flensburg and Magdeburg.

Nolde had needed their understanding and fellowship. Beginning with 1906 the sheer quantity of his production increased considerably. Breaking through Nolde's isolation, the young painters helped him to find his own style as nothing else could have done at that time. Nevertheless he soon retreated to his apartness, rejecting this or any community of artists. He felt that these younger men were still groping, that their group was too closely knit and their paintings all resembled one another; at the time of the 1907 exhibition at the Kunstsalon Richter in Dresden, he remarked that they should "not call themselves Brücke but van Goghiana." [11] He realized that to retain his identity as an artist, he must solve his own problems by himself.

After a series of successful garden pictures, done in dazzlingly brilliant colors, he portrayed himself as *The Free Spirit* (page 16), a large, introverted, proud individual, dressed in a Roman toga, unaffected by the smaller praising, doubting and mocking figures to his left and right. This canvas of 1907 foreshadows his religious paintings in its symbolic content, and its clarity of composition also presages his later work. The four figures — bright red, orange, green and blue — are painted in large flat planes and are firmly constructed. After completing this canvas, however, Nolde turned it to the wall and showed it to no one, possibly realizing that it was not completely successful, for the four figures have a comical aspect not in keeping with the seriousness of his intention.

The Free Spirit. (1907). Oil on canvas, 27¹/₈ x 35″. Nolde Foundation, Seebüll

Nolde now returned for a number of years to painting nature, relying on his spontaneous reaction to pure color rather than on narrative fantasy. He painted garden pieces, cows at pasture, trees or forests, indicating in all of them his love for sensuous color. He wanted almost passively to follow the beckoning of color. Nolde, very prudish in his attitude to life, became a hedonist when writing about color, and he wished to transmit this joy to the viewer.

In his *Wildly Dancing Children* of 1909, the pigment is applied with extraordinary freedom. "The quicker a painting is done, the better it is," [12] he wrote, and forecasting, like Kandinsky, the art of fifty years later: "In art I fight for unconscious creation. Labor destroys painting." [13] The loaded brush went wildly over the canvas as if making its own wriggles and swirls. Colors are extremely bright, with light purples and juicy green predominating. The gay colors, the whirling brush, the exaggerated impressionist dissolution of depth and form create a sweeping joyous movement. For a brief time, Nolde's work seems happy, and unencumbered.

16

Wildly Dancing Children. (1909). Oil on canvas, $28^3/4$ x $34^5/8''$. Kunsthalle zu Kiel

The Last Supper. 1909. Oil on canvas, 34⅝ x 42½".
The Royal Museum of Fine Arts, Copenhagen

The loose and sparkling paintings after nature did not, however, suffice for Nolde's aspirations. In his etchings, woodcuts and lithographs he had first made some fantastic figure compositions of considerable dramatic force. During his entire life he felt a deep personal, almost visionary concern with religion, regarding himself as almost a mystic evangelist. In the summer of 1909, while he was living alone in Ruttebüll in northwestern Schleswig close to his birthplace, he fell severely ill. During this time he experienced a sudden, urgent need for religious self-expression through paintings. "I followed an irresistible desire to represent profound spirituality, religion and tenderness, without much intention, knowledge or deliberation," [14] he recalls in his autobiography.

Although when painting *The Last Supper* Nolde undoubtedly remembered Leonardo's fresco and perhaps even more vividly Rembrandt's *Supper at Emmaus*, this canvas bears little relationship to traditional iconography. Instead he expressed the fervent religious beliefs of the myth-inspired Northern peasantry as well as his own childhood fantasies.

Rembrandt: *Supper at Emmaus*. Musée du Louvre, Paris. Photo Bettmann Archive

Color and light are used evocatively, reaching the greatest climax in the figure of Christ with His glowing yellow face, red robe and hair and white shirt. His personage dominates the scene in light, color and value. The space is crowded and confined. The Apostles with their crude, masklike faces modeled from Frisian fishermen press toward the center, implying a great symbolic embrace. Christ's gesture, too, is in keeping with the general spiritual and mystic content of Nolde's painting. Instead of the dramatic situation represented in Leonardo's mural, when Christ exclaims, "One of ye shall betray me," Nolde shows Christ offering the eucharistic wine, conveying the impression of unity and self-sacrifice.

The Last Supper was followed by the great *Pentecost,* similar in composition and intense emotion. *The Last Supper* and *Pentecost* mark the turning point from external and optical charm to deeply felt inner experience. [15] The following year, still living in the little house in his native marshland and still imbued with Old and New Testament images, Nolde completed no less than ten religious canvases. Among them is the bold *Dance Around the Golden Calf* (page 21), brilliantly colored in strident yellows and blues, and wildly turbulent in its jerky rhythm. Here the story of the Jews' unrestrained worship of the forbidden idol serves as a pretext for painting a sensual and frenzied scene, expressed through movement and color. Nolde's biblical paintings frequently combine a pronounced sensual excitement with his unquestionably sincere religious passions: religion seems, after all, to have been for him a matter of primitive passion, and often he frankly expressed inhibited sexual drives. On the other hand, a rather simple personal color symbolism is the key to the tender *Christ Among the Children* (page 20), formerly in Hamburg's Kunsthalle. Here the tender figure of the Saviour, draped in a blue mantle, looms up protectively as an overpowering diagonal form, separating the bright children

Christ Among the Children. (1910). Oil on canvas, 34$^{1}/_{2}$ x 41$^{7}/_{8}$".
The Museum of Modern Art, New York. Gift of Dr. W. R. Valentiner

— all aglow in red and yellow — from the dark purple disciples, rebuking those who brought the children, dubious and astonished at Christ's concern for them.

Nolde now turned to his most ambitious work, a large nine-part cycle of *The Life of Christ,*[16] related in form and spirit to the late medieval German altarpieces in the church of St. Mary in Flensburg which he had copied with loving emotion and helped restore during his years of apprenticeship. He began this great cycle in Berlin during the winter of 1911-12. It included the rather blurred and pulsating *Christ and Judas,* and the striking panel of *Holy Night* in which Mary, seen in profile much like a figure in an Egyptian wall painting, holds a pink fetal Christ Child in her proudly outstretched arms. There is a large central panel of the *Crucifixion,* with its jagged angular forms and glowing color, and the austere and powerful composition of the *Doubting Thomas.* As the cycle progressed, the forms became simplified, and the vestiges of impressionist technique in the broken color patches were abandoned for firm construction in large areas of separate, symbolic colors, arranged two-dimensionally in broad planes.

Dance Around the Golden Calf. (1910). Oil on canvas, 34⁵/₈ x 41⁵/₈″. Nolde Foundation, Seebüll

ABOVE LEFT: *Mary of Egypt: In the Port of Alexandria.* (1912). Oil on canvas, 33⁷/₈ x 39³/₈″. Kunsthalle, Hamburg

ABOVE CENTER AND OPPOSITE: *Mary of Egypt: The Conversion.* (1912). Oil on canvas, 41³/₈ x 47¹/₄″. Kunsthalle, Hamburg

ABOVE RIGHT: *Mary of Egypt: Death in the Desert.* (1912). Oil on canvas, 33⁷/₈ x 39³/₈″. Kunsthalle, Hamburg

In 1912, he also completed the powerful triptych of *Mary of Egypt,* inspired by the legend of the Alexandrian prostitute who, after seventeen years in her profession, was converted to a chaste life by an image of the Virgin in Jerusalem and became a hermit in the desert across the River Jordan, where she finally died in solitude and was buried by St. Zosimus with the help of a lion. The artist's violent feelings are expressed in this triptych through vibrant gestures and rhythms and, above all, through the blazing reds and yellows. Color pulls the viewer into a picture which is lacking in traditional spatial illusion. But color and gesture are overtly sensuous in the left-hand panel, where the harlot is seen at the height of her powers, flaming like a torch of sensuality among the lustful and vulgar men. Nolde's notions of sensual behavior and attitudes can be primitive almost to the point of caricature. In the central panel Mary, in a vermilion gown with her hair falling in a black cascade, cries out with savage pain in her revelation before the naïvely painted statue of the Virgin. At the right her body has become emaciated, her face peacefully transfigured as she lies dying in the company of the old praying saint and a lion who looks as if he had been borrowed from a children's book.

"In intervals of a few years my pictures with biblical religious content came into existence. The concepts of the small boy, who during the long winter months used to spend all his evenings earnestly reading the Bible, were reawakened. There were pictures of the richest Oriental fantasy. They kept rising in my imagination until the adult man and artist could paint them in dreamlike inspiration." [17]

After a journey to the South Seas, Nolde resumed his biblical subjects in 1915. It was then that he accomplished what is probably his finest painting, the monumental *Entombment.* Here ecstatic excitement has been subdued to deal with the tragedy of death. The two large shapes of Mary and St. Joseph of Arimathea seem to hold Christ's body like a coffin, containing or trying to contain Him. Mary seems to want to take Him back into her womb, but He is much too large for her or for the space that holds Him in the picture. This Christ is not resigned to death but is still struggling: broken-up areas of yellow against the large blue forms create a tension which symbolizes the ultimate tragedy of death. Nolde's great concern with masks at this time may account for St. John's mask of agony, the amazement of Joseph of Arimathea and the tragic suffering of the Christ.

Nolde returned intermittently to biblical subjects in paintings and prints until almost the end of his life. An outstanding later example is *Christ and the Adulteress* of 1926 (page 26) with its golden-yellow glow and stable composition. Its Christ is loving, its mood one of contentment. In *"Be ye as little children"* (page 27), the child is still a romping youngster much like those in the earlier *Christ and the Children,* but the Apostles seem to wear Oceanic masks, while the Christ of the parable is treated as though He were a benevolent and blessing demon.

The Entombment. (1915). Oil on canvas, 33⁷/₈ x 46″. Nolde Foundation, Seebüll

Christ and the Adulteress. (1926). Oil on canvas, 33⁷/₈ x 41³/₄". Dr. Walther Berndorff, Cologne

When Nolde sent his *Pentecost* to the annual exhibition of the Berlin Secession in 1910 it was arrogantly refused, causing a heated public argument. Four years later Max Sauerlandt, the young director of the Halle Museum, bought *The Last Supper,* provoking a pointed censure from Germany's art czar, Wilhelm von Bode. Nolde, who with Rouault and Chagall painted the most significant twentieth-century pictures of explicitly religious subjects, never found acceptance for his work among ecclesiastical authorities. Osthaus, enthusiastic about the large nine-panel *Life of Christ,* exhibited it at an international exposition in Brussels in 1912, only to have it rejected by the Catholic clergy. Nolde then discovered that the Protestant church had little more appreciation for his biblical paintings, mostly because it objected to his use of pronounced Jewish types for Christ and the Apostles. Yet, when a number of his religious paintings, including both the large altarpiece and the triptych of *Mary of Egypt,* were exhibited at St. Catharine's Church in Lübeck in the winter of 1921-22, a reviewer remarked that only when seen in the environment of the big medieval church, with the brilliant colors muted by the diffused light, did they achieve their full, vibrantly glowing effect.[18]

But none of Nolde's religious paintings was ever commissioned, or even permanently installed in a church. With rare exceptions, such as the Dominican church at Assy, the Church of St. Matthew at Northampton in England and the synagogue of the Hebrew University Medical Center near Jerusalem, religious authorities in our time have tended to prefer sweet, or at least "non-controversial," devotional images to powerful and authentic statements about life and its ultimate values, and this was doubtless why no use was found for Nolde's myth-making representation of violence and tragedy.

"Be ye as little children." 1929. Oil on canvas, 41³/₄ x 47¹/₄".
Collection Ernst Henke, Essen

In 1910, when Nolde was already exhibiting all over Germany, he was outraged at having his *Pentecost* rejected by the jury of the Berlin Secession. The entries of the *Brücke* painters were all turned down that same year, and it became quite evident that the powerful Secession, originally founded in the spirit of artistic freedom and once advocating progressive tendencies in painting, was now determined to protect its own vested interests against a new generation.[19] Faced with this situation, Nolde attacked the leadership, appointing himself spokesman for the new generation of German artists.

The Secession was under the direction of Germany's most prominent dealer in contemporary art, Paul Cassirer, and the country's most renowned painter, Max Liebermann. Both men were oriented toward French impressionism and they were both Jewish. Nolde seemed to blame the Jews for his lack of general acceptance during these first ten years of his activities as a painter; his autobiography and letters are filled with the narrow-minded anti-Semitism, nationalism and racism prevalent among the isolated German peasantry and later exploited so successfully by the Nazis. And although his own painting had evolved from impressionism, he now vehemently rejected it in order to affirm his forceful, often brutal kind of art. Admitting that during the nineteenth century Paris had made the greatest contributions to art, he proclaimed that the time had finally arrived for German art to wrest leadership from the French.[20]

No sooner had the leading Berlin art journal *Kunst und Künstler* published an attack upon the young painters, than Nolde took the offensive with an open letter to the Secession's president, Max Liebermann, in which he accused him of dictatorial methods, of personal publicity-seeking, and of bad painting. Naturally this precipitated a public controversy in the Berlin art world. Artists, critics and dealers took sides, and the Secession expelled Nolde. A group calling itself the New Secession under the leadership of Max Pechstein and including all the *Brücke* artists was formed, but most of its members shared neither Nolde's uncompromising attitude nor his provincial chauvinism, and that organization was soon disbanded.

Meanwhile an important exhibition at the Galerie Commeter in Hamburg, directed by the noted archaeologist Botho Graef, proved so successful that some of Nolde's financial worries were solved. In addition he seems actually to have enjoyed the public controversies and now began happy and productive years, in which the summers were spent on Alsen and the winters in Berlin, where he became the rallying point for the new generation of German artists. He participated with them in the great Sonderbund exhibition in Cologne in 1912, which was the first show to manifest the international character of a new type of art. He was visited by a great many artists, including Barlach, Lehmbruck, Beckmann and Marc. In 1912, when the futurists held their show at Walden's Sturm

OPPOSITE: *Master of Ceremonies.* (c. 1911). India ink on Japan paper, 11¹/₂ x 15″. Nolde Foundation, Seebüll

ABOVE LEFT: *A Glass of Wine.* (1911). Oil on canvas, 34⁵/₈ x 28³/₄″. Nolde Foundation, Seebüll

ABOVE RIGHT: *Slovenes.* (1911). Oil on canvas, 31¹/₂ x 27¹/₄″. Nolde Foundation, Seebüll

Still Life of Masks I. (1911). Oil on canvas, 28³/4 x 30¹/2".
Nelson Gallery of Art. Atkins Museum, Kansas City, Mo. (Friends of Art Collection)

gallery, Boccioni and Marinetti called on him. Soon thereafter Otto Freundlich returned from Paris and told him about the new cubist movement. Nolde was sincerely excited by all the new developments in painting and observed how they exerted their influence on most of the German painters of his generation. He was fascinated by the cubist analysis of form, but finally reached the conclusion that "instead of disintegration I sought after cohesion, instead of the breakup of forms I wanted concentration, and in place of taste and technique I searched for deepened expression, broad planes and healthy, strong colors." [21]

During these years Nolde spent only a small part of his time and energy on Berlin art politics, for he became as absorbed in the night life of the metropolis as he had been in the harbor life of Hamburg in 1910. He had always

Candle Dancers. (1912). Oil on canvas, 39³/₈ x 33¹/₂″. Nolde Foundation, Seebüll

loved the dance: he was fascinated by Loïe Fuller and grew to be a close friend of Mary Wigman, the famous exponent of modern dance, whose portrait he painted in watercolor (page 65). He was also greatly attracted to the stage and for a while could be seen almost nightly in Max Reinhardt's famous theater, sketching the most celebrated personalities of the Berlin stage in plays by Shakespeare, Molière, Goethe and Hebbel. He went to the circus, cafés, cabarets and dance halls, sketching singers, dancers, night club impresarios, as well as spectators. These drawings, often catching a quick movement, gesture or glance with a single expressive line, have the vitality of immediate impressions. Their exquisite lightness and sophistication stand in great contrast to most of Nolde's painting and show unexpected versatility.

After setting down these quick impressions, Nolde painted some of the night-life subjects. *A Glass of Wine* of 1911 retains much of the sketchy quality of the drawings and has an astonishing similarity to Kirchner's paintings of the same time — this was the year in which Kirchner moved to Berlin from Dresden. *Slovenes,* also of 1911, is a more carefully executed character study of a rather depraved couple at a café table: a brutish-looking man with a dark face and a grim, despondent lady with a large and most expressive walleye are seated behind a significant still life of bottle and glass. The facial expressions of these individuals, although related in style to the Berlin sketches, seem hardened into masks.

Nolde's use of masks as a theme in his paintings indeed began at about this time. His interest in primitive objects went back to the time he was introduced to them by the *Brücke* artists. But now, early in 1911, he had visited James Ensor in Ostend. Ensor had been using masks as a device for portraying human cruelty and suffering ever since the eighties; unlike his masks, however, Nolde's are never social comments, nor are they satirical. He had neither much interest in society nor much sense of humor. His masks are less literary than Ensor's, and more awesome in their grotesque shapes, symbolic color and savage fantasy.

Nolde's love for the dance, like his interest in the mask, stems from a concern with primitive life and ritual. His paintings of the dance, such as *Wildly Dancing Children, Dance Around the Golden Calf,* and *Candle Dancers,* gave him the chance to make the paint move in the exciting, sinuous patterns he wanted to trace on the canvas. In *Candle Dancers* the entire painting dances: the tall, flickering candles repeat in staccato rhythm the writhing movements of the dancing women. Even the paint dances: the white of the canvas shimmers at intervals among the vibrating reds and yellows of the background and the twisting green and bluish stripes of the women's skirts. The rich pinks of the half-nude bodies leap out startlingly against the shrill Chinese reds and sulphur yellows behind them, and the women's great nipples leap on their breasts like flames. With the vibrant, emotional colors Nolde expresses his own sensuous reactions to this spectacle.

Over the years Nolde's interest in primitive art had constantly grown more intense. He even hoped to publish a book on the art of indigenous peoples, based on his studies in the ethnological museums. He saw in this art, with its abstract and rhythmic sense of ornament and color and its mystic power, an affirmation of his own anti-classical art. He was one of the first artists to protest against the relegation of primitive art objects to anthropological museums, where they were still exhibited as scientific specimens. His own "blood and soil" mystique made him an early proponent of the indigenous art of all peoples.

He was delighted, therefore, to be asked by the German Colonial Ministry to participate as pictorial reporter in an expedition to investigate standards of health in German New Guinea in 1913. The Külz-Leber Expedition, consisting of two physicians, a trained nurse, Nolde and Ada, left Berlin in the early autumn. After traveling by rail across European Russia and Siberia to Manchuria, they sailed to Korea and Japan, where they stayed for three weeks, then across the China Sea back to the Asian continent and Peking, Hankow, Nanking, Shanghai and Hongkong. From there they went on to Manila and the Palau Islands and on to northeastern New Guinea and New Ireland (at that time the German colonies of Kaiser-Wilhelm-Land and Neu-Mecklenburg) and to the Admiralty Islands.

Nolde made sketches at each stage of the journey. There are drawings of patient Russians waiting for days in Siberian railroad stations, of junks sailing the China Sea, of native dancers of New Guinea, as well as idealized and heroic portrait studies of natives. He completed relatively few paintings but made innumerable sketches in pencil and watercolor. He was enthralled with the cohesion of art and life among the aborigines. His long letters, as well as the diary notes for the book *Welt und Heimat*,[22] are full of admiration for the islanders and are highly critical of the European administration's colonial officials, and the missionaries, all of whom he felt exploited the natives: "A magnificent people in so far as they have not already been spoiled by their contact with the white man . . . who is trying to bring the inhabitants of the whole world into servitude."[23]

While Picasso and some of the *Brücke* painters actually changed their styles under the impact of primitive art, thus giving rise to cubism and the mature *Brücke* style, Nolde never made use of the formal aspects of tribal art. Even his masks, though infused with vital intensity, are painted in a completely Western style. He hoped, however, that by absorbing some of the culture of the islanders, he would be able to approach the mystic sources of art and recapture what Jung would call a "racial memory."

During the winter of 1913-14 the Noldes spent six months in Melanesia, where he was sick with tropical diseases for part of the time. They then returned by way of Indonesia, where Nolde loved the rich ornamentation of the Javanese temples,

Nusa lik. (1914). Oil on canvas, 27½ x 41". Museum Folkwang, Essen

and Burma, where he made sketches of the dances. Finally they sailed from Singapore to Port Saïd only to be caught by the declaration of war. Their belongings were seized by the British, but the Noldes themselves managed to return to Germany and the isolated island of Alsen. The canvases Nolde had completed in Melanesia were among the confiscated baggage, and it was not until 1921 that he was able to recover them, in almost miraculously good condition, from the loft of an importer in Plymouth.

Nusa lik, which he painted in New Ireland, was among this group. One of the least representational landscapes Nolde ever painted, it is conceived in large and decorative rhythms of blues and greens. The whole vast lonely scene with its little boats in the small bay and the sea under a bank of clouds is seen from a great height, which accounts for its abstract contours, unusual in Nolde's work.

The impressions of his extensive travels remained with him after his return to Germany, and much of his work was based on the material he had brought back in his sketchbooks. A painting like *Evening Glow,* with the beautiful lyric colors of clouds, water and setting sun, is derived from the studies he made in the China Sea, as well as from actual observation of the sea in the Baltic.

Nolde's new love for Oriental splendor is combined with the intensely personal quality of his religious pictures in *The Ruler* (page 36). The ruler, garbed in his bright yellow robe and striped turban, is seated on his throne, glancing sideways at the viewer with a sly smile. In the background on the left are three soldiers behind

34

bars, while on his right and separated by a definite black vertical line — the painting has the appearance of a diptych — we see two sensuously naked girls from his harem. The space in this painting remains undefined: the girls seem to be in some sort of limbo, yet they continue the colors and lines of the chief, while the soldiers are quite out of focus. Everyone's position — in space and therefore in life — seems to depend on the temper of the ruler, who alone is endowed with real presence.

The character sketches Nolde had made of Russians during his Trans-Siberian journey led to a series of paintings in 1914-15. Perhaps the finest of this group is the *Three Russians* (page 37); their half-length figures are heavily painted, with masklike faces crammed into the frame in regular, rhythmic arrangement like a continuous frieze of heads. Yet there is a sharp distinction of types: the emaciated, ascetic face on the right is in sharp contrast to the other two dark, square, heavier ones — symbols of brutishness and primitive strength.

Evening Glow — South Pacific. (1915). Oil on canvas, 34 x 39¹/₄".
Collection Mr. and Mrs. Donald Winston, Los Angeles

The Ruler. (1914). Oil on canvas, 34⅝ x 40⅛". Galerie Rudolf Hoffmann, Hamburg

Russian II. (c. 1914). Oil on canvas, 26¹/₂ x 23".
Collection Larry Aldrich, New York

Three Russians. 1915. Oil on burlap, 28³/₄ x 39¹/₂".
Collection Mr. and Mrs. David Bakalar, Boston

After his return from the South Pacific Nolde relied increasingly on emotional expressions intensified by his feeling for color. Although he hated all categories and wrote: "Intellectuals and literati call me an expressionist. I do not like this narrow classification. A German artist, that I am." [24] He was indeed recognized as a founder and leader of the expressionist movement. He may be so regarded if expressionism can be defined as a probing search for a deep emotional reality behind appearances — a reality that the artist finds by observing his own subjective reactions, and for which he then fashions an adequate and equivalent formal means to evoke a similar response in the viewer.

Nolde set out to paint a scene as it must feel from inside it. His response to the ocean was particularly acute. He was born on the edge of the sea and all his life he chose to live close to it. His brief stay in Hamburg in 1910 brought about not only a group of superb drawings, woodcuts and etchings, but generated also a series of splendid oils of tugboats and steamships in which the color itself communicates the life of the harbor, its feel and smell, and its atmosphere of water, clouds and diffused light. He tells of a violent crossing of the Kattegat which took place at about this time. The small boat was tossed angrily with each wave. "This day," he says, "has remained so fixed in my memory, that for years afterwards all my paintings of the sea consisted of wildly heaving green waves and only a little edge of yellow sky on the upper fringe." [25]

The experience gave rise to a long series of pictures in which the ocean is no longer seen from a distance as in traditional seascapes, including Nolde's own early *Moonlit Night* (page 12). These paintings, with their surging bottle-green waves and sparkling, heaving whitecaps, the dark valleys between the crests, the low horizons and sometimes strange sweeping cloud formations are more than depictions of the sea. They are visual equivalents of a physical experience. It is as if the painter were saying: "This is what it feels like to be tossed about in the sea." Usually the pictures of autumnal seas are close-up views, limited to waves and sky. Occasionally boats appear, as in the recollections of the China Sea of 1915 or in a painting, such as *Fishing Boat* of one year later. But no safe shore line is ever indicated. The sea was for Nolde the embodiment of a regenerative primordial force, always changing and never tame — an element of ominous power. He continued painting the ocean until the very end of his long life, but over the years his seascapes became less tempestuous, more quiet, and a soft light becomes an increasingly important element in them. In *Luminous Sea* (page 40), one of his last paintings, a diffuse light dematerializes the seascape in a manner reminiscent of the late work of Turner, its still mood and fusion of sea and sky suggesting infinity.

The Sea III. (1913). Oil on canvas, 34 x 39³/₈″. Nolde Foundation, Seebüll

Luminous Sea. (1948). Oil on canvas, 26³/₄ x 34⁵/₈″. Nolde Foundation, Seebüll

The Evening (Marsh Landscape). (1916). Oil on canvas, 29 x 39⁵/₈". Kunstmuseum, Basel

During the twenties and thirties Nolde continued to spend his winters in Berlin and to take an active part in the artistic and intellectual life of the metropolis. He exhibited widely, by this time being recognized as a major force in modern art. His paintings were entering the chief museums. In 1921 Max Sauerlandt published an important monograph on his work, and in 1927, on the occasion of his sixtieth birthday, a large retrospective exhibition of over two hundred paintings was arranged by Rudolf Probst in Dresden and later shown in Hamburg, Kiel, Essen and Wiesbaden. In 1931 he was finally elected to membership in the Prussian Academy of Fine Arts and the same year he published the first part of his memoirs, to be followed by a second volume three years later. There is no doubt that Nolde enjoyed his status as a public figure and that he needed and loved the excitement of the capital and the various stimuli it offered. But late in the spring he always returned to the north country, and it was there that all his significant later canvases were executed.

He had left his little fisherman's shack on the island of Alsen in 1916 for small quarters in the village of Utenwarf close to his birthplace. When after World War I this area joined Denmark, Nolde became a Danish citizen, remaining a Dane until his death. In 1926, however, he acquired land on the German side of the border, where he began building his own house and studio, calling it Seebüll. He and Ada found the particular spot after extensive searching, largely on foot, along the whole coast of Schleswig-Holstein. Here the artist designed a strange, six-cornered brick building of no particular style, too heavy for the landscape which it dominates like a castle, but whose unconventional plan was precisely what he needed and wanted. There he spent his long summers until 1941, and the entire year throughout the remainder of his life.

In Utenwarf and Seebüll, in this rather desolate and lonely northern countryside, he executed some of the most powerful landscapes of the twentieth century, landscapes that speak of the vast spaces and the great quiet of the moors, where the ever-changing light and restless clouds give drama and life to nature. Long stretches of marshland with low horizons appear in *The Evening,* in which a jagged, grey cloudscape dominates the lonely green marsh, and the viewer is pulled along the winding path toward a distant center where a sulphur yellow sky and a distant blue mountain range beckon. He painted clouds which sweep across the sky like the threatening finger of a mighty hand, intimidating young horses. In *Sultry Evening* he superimposes a huge bunch of flowers on a fantastic landscape. The flowers do not relieve the frightening aspect of the scene, with its orange cloud looming out of the green sky and surmounting the low-lying black cloud that enshrouds the farmhouse; its blazing color threatens the spectator like an eerie manor in Gothic tales, but with far more effective simplicity of statement. He made pictures of the mills which dot the countryside, but communicate a feeling of mystery, as in *Nordermühle* (page 44), where no wind animates the arms of the mill, and no human being enters the portentous scene. A burning orange and yellow

Sultry Evening. (1930). Oil on canvas, 28³/₄ x 39³/₈″. Nolde Foundation, Seebüll

Nordermühle. (1932). Oil on canvas, 28³/₄ x 34⁵/₈". Bayerische Staatsgemäldesammlungen, Munich

The Great Gardener. (1940). Oil on canvas, 27¹/₂ x 22"
Collection Dr. Bernhard Sprengel, Hanover

cloud is reflected in the silent pool, and the still water seems to be smoldering with a sulphurous flame. He loved the mysterious mood: in *Frisian Farm on a Canal* (page 48), mostly composed of the saturated green of the moorland and the rich ultramarine blue of the sky, two small light clouds and the glowing yellow haystack only underline the mood of heavy solemnity.

   This painting was made in 1935, when Nolde had been gravely ill for some time with cancer of the stomach. He now underwent surgery, and the mood of his work became less forbidding after the successful operation.

Ripe Sunflowers. (1932). Oil on canvas, 29 x 35". The Detroit Institute of Arts

Great Poppies — Red, Red, Red. (1942). Oil on canvas, 28³/₄ x 34¹/₂″. Nolde Foundation, Seebüll

Frisian Farm on a Canal. (1935). Oil on canvas, 28³/₄ x 34⁵/₈". Nolde Foundation, Seebüll

In addition to the northern ocean and marshland, Nolde always loved flowers. Poor as he was, he planted a luxurious flower garden next to his little hut in Alsen. When he moved his summer quarters to Utenwarf, he grew another garden (they were unknown to the farmers in the coastal regions until that time). Finally, when he had erected Seebüll, he planted a lush flower garden in that bleak countryside and filled it with sunflowers, amaryllis, roses, poppies, even camellias. The flower beds themselves were arranged to form the initials "A" and "E" for Ada and Emil (Nolde's taste was a peculiar combination of middle-class banality and unique individuality); this garden served as his model for a great many oils and watercolors during the last thirty years of his life.

The garden pictures of 1906 were the first really successful group of paintings. He recalls: "It was in midsummer. The colors of the flowers attracted me irresistibly and at once I was painting. My first flower pictures came into being." [26] In them he began to approach color for its own sake, and it was these paintings which appealed to the *Brücke* painters as "tempests of color," causing them to invite him to membership. The dramatic quality of these pictures, still impressionist, was soon enhanced. He became less interested in the effect of light, working in the shade in order to see color most clearly without the diffusion of sunlight, and by about 1913 color has overcome other elements in the garden pictures. They resemble tapestries in which massed flat areas of color are placed in a rhythmic arrangement. At times he strove for a great brilliance of color; at others a dark, subdued, almost ominous mood prevails. Here, even more than in his other oils, color is the basis for his form and does in fact create an order following its own needs. He was also fond of including flowers in his still lifes, combining a bouquet with Melanesian masks, Burmese carvings, Chinese idols or other items from his variegated collection of exotic objects. This mélange of oddities often lends a strange, almost surreal flavor to the familiar flowers themselves.

But his finest flower pictures are removed from all environmental relationships. Like the waves seen without coastlines, they are painted without soil or vase. Nolde presents us only with petals, stamens, pistils and perhaps a few leaves. These he humanizes with his own emotion: "The blossoming colors of the flowers and the purity of those colors — I love them. I loved the flowers and their fate: shooting up, blooming, radiating, glowing, gladdening, bending, wilting, thrown away and dying." [27]

It took considerable boldness for a painter who admired van Gogh [28] as much as Nolde did to paint sunflowers, yet he often returned to them and added a new and rich interpretation to the motif. *Ripe Sunflowers* of 1937 is an impassioned painting of the flowers in full bloom. These blossoms are large, engulfing, womblike creations, but they are also already marked with the sign of death as the heavy flowers bend with their own weight, soon to lose their seeds, which they will no longer be able to hold.

In a much happier moods is *Great Poppies — Red, Red, Red* of 1942, one of the few pictures he dared paint during the Nazi persecution. The Whistlerian subtitle suggests that Nolde was concerned primarily with the pure play of color: vermilion, pink and purple. These flowers, beautifully composed within the picture frame, stand up against the elements with a fresh, windswept vitality.

At times Nolde would also set personages in his gardens. *In the Lemon Grove* is a modern allegory on the theme of love, expressed of course by means of color. *The Great Gardener* of 1940 resembles a quiet poem about the mystery of creation: the naïvely conceived God — the German *Lieber Gott*, bearded, kind, benevolent — tends His garden, fructifying a miraculously tall orange flower which grows toward Him like a burning chalice.

Flower Garden. (c. 1913). Oil on canvas, 28³/₄ x 34³/₄″. Collection Mr. and Mrs. Morton D. May, St. Louis

Nolde, who came to occupy the top rank among twentieth-century printmakers, had begun etching in 1898. His first important group of etchings — a series of grotesques and fairy-tale fantasies — was made in 1904, about four years before his work in oil shows a similar richness of imagination. At times certain compositions appear years earlier in Nolde's prints than in his paintings, but in a good many instances the painted version precedes the graphic one. Yet in every instance, the peculiar characteristics of the medium had a determining effect on the final products. "I want my work to grow from the material, just as in nature the soil from which it grows determines the character of the plant," Nolde wrote in 1906.[29]

His early etchings were still soft and rather diffuse, showing an influence from impressionism much like that in his early painting style. In other prints, especially of nudes, the decorative, sinuous line indicates a derivation from art nouveau. Soon, however, he developed a unique and personal technique which, though achieved by pure etching, gives his prints an effect similar to aquatint. In these his interest in tonal values rather than in line determined the results. As early as 1906 Gustav Schiefler, the collector and connoisseur of prints, while working on the definitive catalog of Edvard Munch's graphic work, was attracted by Nolde's etchings and became their first important collector. Soon thereafter Schiefler wrote the first comprehensive essay on Nolde and as early as 1911 published a definitive catalog of his prints to date, following it with a second volume in 1927.[30]

When in 1906 Nolde joined the *Brücke,* he was already an accomplished etcher, and while he was teaching his friends about etching, they in turn introduced him to the woodcut.[31] He was fascinated with this printing technique, mastering it quickly because of his early training in wood carving, and he completed his first series of about thirty woodcuts that same year. These woodcuts show the influence of Munch as much as that of the *Brücke* painters. A comparison of Nolde's early woodcuts with those of Kirchner reveals the contrast between the two rather than their similarities. As a colorist, Nolde is concerned with light and dark values and their planar relationships, whereas Kirchner surrenders himself to the free arabesque of linear movement. In his woodcuts Nolde gave free rein to his imagination. In *The Large Bird* (page 56), an awkward little girl stolidly confronts a monstrous gloomy bird, flapping his big wings; the enormous bird — itself a rather threatening image — seems frightened by the girl. It suggests some strange legend of a bird, pursued by a child much smaller than itself, neither aware of its own power and strength. Six years after having made this woodcut, which perhaps was known to Munch when he did his lithograph *Omega and the Bear* in the *Omega Series* of 1908—09, Nolde did a highly effective painting of the same fantasy, now in the Royal Museum of Fine Arts, Copenhagen.

In 1910 Nolde went to Hamburg where, enthralled by the harbor, he made a group of superb India-ink drawings with a dry brush (page 62), as well as woodcuts and etchings (pages 54,56). These prints are not as subjective in content as the earlier (or later) series; he was thoroughly excited by the visual stimulus of the industrial landscape, the port with its barges, tenders, tugs and docks, and its waves and smoke. During the day he sketched and drew in a small boat, and at night in his sailor's hostel he etched his plates with furious speed, placed them in the acid, lay down to sleep for a few hours, and awoke in time to remove them from the bath. Sometimes he seems to have used double biting for the deepest lines. These etchings of Hamburg harbor with their network of brittle lines capture the vital atmosphere of the port as it was experienced in the artist's highly stimulated imagination. They also show his enjoyment of the medium and the rich inventiveness of his technique. The woodcuts of identical subjects are simpler and harder, as one would expect. Like the ink drawings, to which they are related, they are also reminiscent of Far Eastern art in their large and emblematic calligraphic forms.

The prints of Hamburg were followed in 1911 by a series of religious etchings, such as *Solomon and His Wives*, *Saul and David* and *Scribes* (page 55), revealing

Reclining Woman. 1908. Etching and aquatint, printed in green, 12¹/₈ x 18⁵/₈″. (Sch. R 92 III/III). The Museum of Modern Art, New York. Purchase

Nude. (1906). Etching, 7¹¹/₁₆ x 5⁵/₈″. (Sch. R 34, II, a).
Nolde Foundation, Seebüll

The Artist's Wife. (1911). Drypoint, 9¹/₁₆ x 7³/₁₆″.
(Sch. R 165 III/III).
The Museum of Modern Art, New York. Purchase

Flood. (1922). Etching, 9⁷/₈ x 16¹⁵/₁₆″. (Sch. R 223, III).
Nolde Foundation, Seebüll

Hamburg Harbor. 1910. Etching and aquatint, 12¹/₁₆ x 16¹/₈″.
(Sch. R 137). Collection Mr. and Mrs. E. Powis Jones, New York

Scribes. (1911). Etching and aquatint, printed in brown-black, 10¹/₂ x 11³/₄".
(Sch. R 154 II/II). The Museum of Modern Art, New York. Purchase

the same fantastic and mystic vision that gives such force to his religious paintings.
"My etchings," he wrote, "do not belong to some kind of art that can be enjoyed
from a comfortable easy chair . . . they demand that the viewer leap drunkenly
with them." [32]

He sought a similar effect in the series of powerful woodcuts of 1912. *The
Prophet* (page 57) from this group is startling at first glance because of the large
areas of black, but the white sections are actually those that receive chief emphasis.
Broken by black lines an inch or half an inch in thickness, these white areas are
largely concentrated in the center of the picture. The gaunt cheekbones, the retina
of the left eye, the stubborn lower lip, the high, sloping bony forehead — these
areas, besides being effective because of their central position, are also easily read
as symbols: they are traditionally associated with the prophet. Like a legendary
mask, this disembodied head floats into the picture and gives the print some of the
dramatic intensity and the heavy monumentality of an icon. Although as a graphic

medium the more painterly lithography was to occupy his chief interest and attention after 1911, Nolde continued to work in both etching and woodcut. In 1917, in fact, he completed another fine set of woodcuts, including the rather savage print, *The Family*. These are freer in form than the earlier prints, and the artist's inclination toward the broadly conceived plane finds the woodcut technique particularly congenial.

The last series of etchings, done in 1918 and 1922 — grotesques and fantasies as well as landscapes — shows an increasing graphic sensibility, a new delicacy of technique and a mastery of the material which results in infinite variations of greys and beautifully textured surfaces of organic richness.

As early as his Munich period in the nineties, Nolde made an attentive study of Daumier's lithographs, fascinated by their tension and large planes of light and shade. Perhaps he had seen and admired Daumier's prints even earlier; his caricatures of Swiss types would certainly suggest such a possibility.

It was also while in Munich that Nolde first became familiar with the technical process of lithography. In 1907 he made his first series of thirty-one lithographs, drawing the faces and figures of music-hall dancers with India ink on tracing paper and simply using the stone for multiplication of the design — a procedure that was customary at the time. But it was not until 1913 that he really learned about the medium, when in a lithography workshop in Flensburg he was given complete freedom among the stones and presses. Like Picasso at Mourlot's in 1947, Nolde was enthralled with the medium, realizing that "the painter can experience the fascination of the technique and its far-reaching possibilities only when he himself works creatively on the stone."[33]

He loved the possibilities of stones for various colors and at times used as many as five, indeed expanding the limits of color lithography by making huge prints which combine a powerful color symbolism with the flatness peculiar to the graphic medium. He constantly experimented with different states and variations: *Young Couple* (page 58) exists in seventy-two printings.[34] This print, *The Three Kings, Discussion, Mother and Child,* and the magnificent *Dancer* (page 59), while lacking the often brutal roughness of the oils, have an emotional appeal equal to that of his work in any medium. His feeling about human encounters as sacred, spiritual or magical events are evoked by color and plane as well as by expressive gesture. As a unit, Nolde's thirteen color lithographs of 1913 constitute the climax of German expressionist graphic art.

Nolde returned once more to color lithography in 1926, now eliminating the black stone entirely. In keeping with the general development of his work in the twenties, these large prints, while lacking the dramatic agitation of the earlier lithographs, are handled more broadly. They have an effect of great peace, and, at times, as in *The Sea* done in the late twenties, achieve monumentality.

Owing partly to a weakening of his eyesight, Nolde gave up his work as a printmaker in his sixties; this coincided with his greatest concentration upon the fluid medium of watercolor.

TOP: *The Large Bird*. (1906). Woodcut, 6¹/₂ x 8⁵/₁₆". (Sch. H 9, III). Nolde Foundation, Seebüll

Fishing Boat. (1910). Woodcut, 12 x 15³/₄". (Sch. H 34). Nolde Foundation, Seebüll

Prophet. (1912). Woodcut, 12⁵/₈ x 8³/₄". (Sch. H 110).
The Museum of Modern Art, New York. Given Anonymously

Family. (1917). Woodcut, 9⁷/₁₆ x 12⁵/₈".
(Sch. H 128, II). Nolde Foundation, Seebüll

Young Couple. (1913). Lithograph, printed in color from three stones,
24⁷/₁₆ x 20¹/₁₆″. (Sch. L 52, DII/E, sixth variation). The Museum of Modern
Art, New York. Mrs. John D. Rockefeller, Jr. Purchase Fund.

Dancer. 1913. Lithograph, printed in color, 21^1/$_{16}$ x 27^1/$_8$". (Sch. L 56).   Collection Mrs. Gertrud A. Mellon, New York

Expressionism may be described as the utterance of the artist's subjective emotion; expressionists generally are not particularly concerned with problems of structure or composition. Kandinsky, Nolde's most important contemporary, and pioneer among the abstract expressionists in Germany, insisted that form must be nothing but the outgrowth of the artist's "inner necessity." The best expressionist paintings are those in which this direct and instinctive approach strikes home without the intervention of rational thought. Nolde was quite aware of the need for spontaneity, although he placed more emphasis on the act of seeing and never turned to pure abstraction: "I have found it difficult, after having reached the creative climax in my work — something that happened rather early in the process — to sustain the tension until it was completed. When the pure sensual force of seeing weakens, rational coldness can take over, leading to a slackening and even destruction." [35]

Because of the great importance of immediacy in Nolde's creative process, he found watercolor an ideal medium. Here no change was possible, and there was no need for a prolonged translation from imagination to formal structure. In his analytical remarks about his work he continues: "I could imagine my work down to the smallest detail, and my concept was usually much more beautiful than the finished work. I became the copyist of my own conception. It is for that reason that I try to avoid all thinking. A vague concept of color and luminosity suffices, and the picture evolves during the act of painting." [36]

His first fully realized work was a minute watercolor ($3\frac{1}{2}$ x 4 inches) of a mountain sunrise of 1894 (opposite) while he was still in Switzerland. He was quite aware that "it indicated a direction, because it made me so happy. But I was unable to turn out another picture of this kind. Did I already suspect that the long road from joy in nature, externally perceived and described — as in all my preceding landscapes in watercolor — would ultimately lead me to artistically free concepts that came wholly from within?" [37]

It took him over a decade to continue along the direction anticipated in this small watercolor. It was not until his brief stay near Jena in 1908 that he was able to achieve a similarly strong and evocative feeling in a group of glowing watercolors. Again he was working under trying conditions. He had failed with a group of oils; it was extremely cold, yet he felt he must work outdoors, and he turned to watercolor, sometimes sitting in the snow and using pieces of ice to paint with. "At times I also painted in the freezing evening hours and was glad to see the frozen colors turn into crystal stars and rays on the paper. I loved this collaboration with nature, yes, the whole natural alliance of painter, reality and picture." [38] Thus as early as 1908 he was letting the material speak for itself and welcoming the element of chance: the traces of ice crystals formed by the frozen watercolor are still visible in the lower margin of *Sunset*.

Before Sunrise. (1894). Watercolor, 3¹/₄ x 4″. Nolde Foundation, Seebüll

Sunset. 1908. Watercolor, 14¹/₄ x 19¹/₄″. Nolde Foundation, Seebüll

BELOW LEFT: *Steamer on the Elbe.* (1910). Pen and wash, 13¹/₈ x 9⁷/₈". Wallraf-Richartz-Museum, Cologne

BELOW RIGHT: *Chinese Junk.* (c. 1914). Watercolor, 10³/₄ x 12¹/₂". Collection Mr. and Mrs. Eugene Victor Thaw, New York

Kurland. Watercolor, 13³/₈ x 18⁵/₈".
Städtische Galerie im Landesmuseum, Hanover

North Sea. Watercolor, 13¹/₄ x 17⁷/₈". Nolde Foundation, Seebüll

ABOVE LEFT: *Head of an Apostle*. (1909). Watercolor, 13¾ x 11¼". Kunsthalle, Hamburg

ABOVE RIGHT: *South-Sea Island Chief*. (c. 1913). Watercolor, 19 x 13⅝". Collection Dr. G. Thiem, Hanover

OPPOSITE LEFT: *Self Portrait*. Watercolor, 18½ x 13⅞". Nolde Foundation, Seebüll

OPPOSITE RIGHT: *Portrait of Mary Wigman*. (c. 1920). Watercolor, 19 x 15". Collect. Mr. and Mrs. Jos. M. Edinburg, Chestnut Hill, Mass.

Red Poppies. Watercolor, 13 x 18″. Collection Mr. and Mrs. Hans Popper, San Francisco

The following years in a state of great excitement, he began working again with watercolor, or rather wash and pencil on paper, in studies for heads of the Apostles for *The Last Supper* (page 64). In 1910 he did his telling interpretations of Hamburg harbor with a dry brush and India ink (page 62), and in 1911 he turned to watercolor and a thin brush for his quick, delightful renditions of Berlin night life (pages 28, 68).

He found watercolor most useful for rapid sketches on his trip to the South Seas in 1913. He executed a group of extraordinary watercolors of Chinese junks which, although using Western illusionistic space, are nevertheless strongly reminiscent of Oriental art, not merely in their subject matter but in the astonishing certainty of the dashing line, in their economy of means, and in the definite emblematic appearance of the black shapes and their disposition on the page.

In New Guinea he made a number of portraits of aborigines, lending them the nobility of native deities. Nolde quite clearly continued to be imbued with romantic faith in the Noble Savage.

A number of watercolors of the Northern landscape, many of which were executed in Utenwarf, were done on non-absorbent paper whose whiteness served as the white of the picture. After applying the color, Nolde would add strong and decorative black outlines which animate the composition (page 63, top).

But after his trip to the Orient, and possibly slightly earlier, he also used a different technique which he pushed to a highly advanced point. Employing an absorbent Japan paper, he moistened it and then applied the watercolor, permitting the pigments to flow into each other, controlling their movement with a tuft of cotton. There is no white, only color. This new use of watercolor was his innovation, necessary to permit him the free improvisations he desired. Often — almost as in a Rorschach ink blot — the configuration on the wet page would suggest a cloud, a mountain, the sea or a flower, from which the artist would capture and articulate the vision.

These watercolors are impossible to date. Chronological classification seemed pedantic and unnecessary to Nolde, for he once told Fehr: "To the annoyance of art historians I shall destroy all lists that give information about the dates of my pictures." [39] In view of this attitude, it is amusing as well as helpful that a precise catalog of his oils was kept by Ada Nolde and, after her death, by Joachim von Lepel, as director of the Nolde Foundation. Unfortunately, however, this list did not include the thousands of watercolors, and as there is little stylistic or thematic change after about 1920, it is impossible to assign specific dates to most of them. The only alteration which seems apparent is that in the late sheets he used an even easier and softer transition between color areas and a spotty technique within individual areas, giving them an organic appearance of fungi or lichens that he had earlier achieved only in the etchings.

The themes of the watercolors vary little from the oils. He was fascinated by the skies, the drama of light and dark performed by the clouds. There are many close-ups of flowers, some beautifully decorative, some with heavily symbolic

Singer. (c. 1911). Watercolor, 12^1/$_2$ x 8^3/$_4$".
Kunsthalle, Hamburg

sexual overtones; his figure pieces, increasing in number over the years, are also preoccupied with the male-female relationship.

The watercolors range from the lightest transparency to deep and full opacity, from the firm structure of the usually earlier ones with their heavy outlines to the more fluid later pictures. They have become the most accessible and therefore the most popular of his works, but perhaps they are also the most fully resolved. Nolde elevated watercolor far above the level of a specialized technique and achieved works of a breathtaking and ephemeral beauty which stand unique in the history of twentieth-century art. They remain unencumbered by the occasional awkward handling of pastose paint but rather convey by a light directness the spontaneity with which they were done. In this wet-on-wet technique Nolde welcomes the accident, he controls it, and anticipates a later generation of "informal" painters, some of whom surely felt the impact of his work.

The watercolor of the very dramatically conceived figures of early 1932 was created during one night when NOLDE suddenly jumped out of bed and in his dressing gown ran into his atelier to get freed of the vision of figures in which he symbolized the love of his very own happiness. His wife Ada was amazed by the sudden awakening of Emil, and she told me in his presence that when the composition of the two figures was finished, he took a deep breath and said to her, "This is our best portrait of our superior being". And then, she added, "Emil worked as though obsessed and he refused to sit down and have breakfast as he could not leave the picture until it was finished."

from a letter ISO BRANTE SCHWEIDE to Ala Story,
Valla de Bravo, Mexico.　　　　July 15, 1957.

The Lovers (Self Portrait of the Artist with His Wife). (1932).
Watercolor, 13$^{1}/_{2}$ x 19$^{1}/_{2}$".
Collection Mrs. Ala Story, Santa Barbara

"Blood and Soil," "Art and Race," and similar cultural propaganda slogans trumpeted by the Nazis could not fail to appeal to Emil Nolde, whose own position was consistently that of a pan-German chauvinist. National identity has always been a highly sensitive matter among the Germans. But a feeling of national insecurity is apt to run especially high among the border populations, like those of South Tyrol, the Sudetenland, and the Baltic, as well as North Schleswig. In addition, Nolde felt that all great art had to be "indigenous to the race," which accounts to a considerable extent for his admiration of primitive art. His own position as a German artist, as we have seen, had been consistently anti-French and anti-Jewish. He was, however, thoroughly inexperienced politically, and when Hitler and his supporters proclaimed the German National Revolution of 1933 Nolde naïvely expected to become a part, and indeed the artistic spearhead, of "The Movement."

He was soon to be deeply disillusioned. The petty-bourgeois taste of Hitler himself prevailed against all aspects of modernism, and Nolde in particular was singled out for attack as a "degenerate artist" and "cultural bolshevik." His friends among the German museum directors, including his champion Max Sauerlandt, were dismissed from their positions as soon as the Nazis took power, and Nolde's own work began to disappear from the walls of museums. An exhibition of his work was closed by the Gestapo. In the Degenerate Art exhibition in Munich in 1937 the Nazi art officials mockingly displayed twenty-seven of his works together with those of most other important modern artists. Soon all his paintings not in his own or other private hands were seized, and some were sold at auction in Switzerland. Unlike most of his contemporaries at work in Germany — artists such as Albers, Beckmann, Feininger, Grosz, Kandinsky, Klee, and Kokoschka — Nolde did not emigrate. As a Danish subject he could not have been prevented from leaving the country, but he could not conceive of giving up his beloved Seebüll, and in any case he still had faith in the eventual acceptance of his German art by the National Socialist government. He continued to petition the authorities and even took new hope when his local chapter of an organization of German nationalists in North Schleswig was absorbed into the Nazi party in 1940. Yet in the summer of 1941 he was ruthlessly informed that: "In view of the Führer's decree concerning the elimination of degenerate art from the museums, 1052 of your works have been confiscated . . . . For your lack of reliability you are expelled from the Board of National Culture and are as of this instant forbidden from exercising any professional or avocational activity in the fine arts." [40]

When Nolde wrote to his friend Hans Fehr about this annihilating decree, he nevertheless still expressed his hope and faith in Germany's victory in the war. Still he did not wholly obey the interdiction, but secretly painted many very small watercolors, the "Unpainted Pictures." As late as 1942 he made a final attempt to appeal to Nazi officialdom, traveling to Vienna to see Austria's *Gauleiter*, Baldur von Schirach, only to be rejected once more. To add to his misfortune, his Berlin studio was totally burned in an Allied air raid in 1943, and all his etching plates, woodblocks and lithography stones as well as about three thousand prints and drawings were destroyed. At the same time he was anxiously concerned over the whereabouts and condition of all his confiscated paintings — the creative endeavor of a lifetime.

Nevertheless, sitting in a small room in Seebüll during the years of Nazi persecution and using very small pieces of paper, he painted hundreds of watercolors. These he called "Ideas for Paintings" or "Unpainted Pictures." As in the earlier watercolors he allowed wet paint to flow over the wet paper, and again the old artist's trained eye and matured imagination spontaneously caught the images suggested by the fluid color. But unlike larger watercolors, the Unpainted Pictures are denser in their composition. Their much smaller size — usually only about eight by six inches — and the fact that they were intended as studies for oil paintings necessitated this change toward a more definite condensation.

These multitudes of small papers are only now beginning to be known. There are still occasional landscapes, but almost all of them deal with the human figure. Many look almost like specific illustrations to unwritten stories. But the only fable that is illustrated by these untitled watercolors is Nolde's own fantasy, the imagination of a storyteller whose images emerge from ancient myth and personal fantasy.

Many years before Nolde turned to these strange little pictures, on the occasion of his sixtieth birthday, his close friend Paul Klee had written: "... In their divorce or flight from earth, abstractionists sometimes forget Nolde's existence. Not so I, even on my remotest flights from which I always return in order to rest with a newly discovered weight. Nolde is more than only bound to the earth. He is also a demon of the lower earthly regions. Yet, even from another sphere, one senses in him a cousin of the depths, but a cousin by election .... His hand is a creative human hand, not without heaviness, which writes in a script not without flaws, the mysterious full-blooded hand of the lower regions .... The heart of creation beats for all and nourishes all spheres." [41]

But now at last the hand of the old painter works "without heaviness." By this time Nolde had learned much about human relationships, and in this great cycle he gave a passionate visual form to his wisdom. There are figures that appeal, reject, wail, smile and contemplate. There are lonely people, jealous people, alienated individuals who wish to form contacts but are unable to do so. This world is peopled with beautiful and desirable young women, blindly groping old men, grimacing gnomes and compassionate demons. Again we see combinations of man and flower as well as disputations between the most unlikely antagonists. The imagination here often recalls the *dramatis personae* of *The Tempest, Peer Gynt* or Munch's anxious fantasies, although it is much less perturbed than that of Munch. Indeed, Nolde's private world has been transfigured into a serene

Old Man with Beard. Watercolor and gouache on Japan paper, $10^{1}/_{2}$ x 9". Nolde Foundation, Seebüll

realm of human actors whose chief function is their subservience to the color which gave them birth.

The colors are still "tempestuous" but no longer aggressive. Instead they now have the full resonance that occurs at times in the work of masters in their old age. The colors and the figures to whom they have given form pursue Nolde's interest in the dualities of human relationship. He asks here the same time-worn questions so often asked by creative artists: How do the sexes face each other? What is the relationship between old age and youth, tragedy and joy, good and evil? How does man confront society? Which is reality and which the mask? But all these questions have become visual questions and are expressed with "ability, fantasy and visual power," the three virtues Nolde postulated for great art during his student days in Munich.

After the bitter and frustrating years of Nazism and war, Nolde emerged as the grand old man of German art. But in 1946 his wife Ada, long an invalid, died of a heart attack. To combat his loneliness the aged painter became engaged to the twenty-six-year-old Jolanthe Erdmann, daughter of his friend, the pianist Eduard Erdmann, and was married to her in 1948. He continued painting, translating some of his Unpainted Pictures into oils (page 74). His colors were more subdued now and he shunned the contrast of complementaries which he had liked so much in his earlier, more vigorous days. His final paintings have a softened quality; their mood is serene and contemplative. A diffuse, liquid light was added to his vocabulary and became, indeed, an essential element (page 40).

In 1952 a great celebration honoring his eighty-fifth birthday took place in Seebüll, where distinguished friends from all over Germany, Denmark and Switzerland mingled with his peasant relatives. He was now decorated and bemedaled, given an honorary professorship, awarded important national and international prizes and large retrospective exhibitions. He could finally look back on the rich accomplishments of a fertile life.

His last oils are dated in his eighty-fifth year, and he continued painting water-colors almost until his death on April 13th, 1956, at the age of eighty-eight.

Always reluctant to part with his paintings, which he and Ada considered their children, Nolde had retained a very large number of his oils, watercolors and prints, including many of the most important works. These he left in permanent trust to the Nolde Foundation, administered after his death under the capable and loving direction of his devoted friend, the late Joachim von Lepel. The studio-house of Seebüll has now become the Nolde Museum and is a fitting memorial to a great painter. There in Nolde's own countryside, which was so essential to his art, the visitor can concentrate in quiet contemplation upon the unique pictorial language Nolde created: a language which endowed the mystical spirit of the North and a turbulent personal fantasy with a command of color, unprecedented in its power.

ABOVE LEFT: *Circus People*. Watercolor and gouache on
Japan paper, 8³⁄₈ x 7⁵⁄₈". Nolde Foundation, Seebüll

LEFT: *Little Faun*. Watercolor and gouache on
Japan paper, 9 x 5⁵⁄₈". Nolde Foundation, Seebüll

ABOVE RIGHT: *Bird Over Mountains*. Watercolor and
gouache on Japan paper, 9 x 6". Nolde Foundation, Seebüll

ABOVE: *Girls from Far Away*. 1947. Oil on canvas, 26³/₄ x 34⁵/₈".
Kunsthalle, Mannheim

LEFT: *Girls from Far Away*. Watercolor and gouache on
Japan paper, 6³/₄ x 10³/₄". Nolde Foundation, Seebüll

The Passer-by. Watercolor and gouache on Japan paper,
9³/₄ x 6⁵/₈". Nolde Foundation, Seebüll

NOTES

[1] Nolde, *Das eigene Leben*, Berlin, Rembrandt Verlag, 1931, p. 152.

[2] Nolde, *Jahre der Kämpfe*, Berlin, Rembrandt Verlag, 1934, p. 62.

[3] Nolde, *Das eigene Leben*, p. 127.

[4] Nolde, letter to Hans Fehr, Dachau, May 7, 1889, in Hans Fehr, *Nolde*, Cologne, DuMont Schauberg, 1957, p. 23.

[5] *Ibid.*

[6] Nolde, *Das eigene Leben*, p. 144.

[7] Nolde, letter to Hans Fehr, Friedenau, March 5, 1909, in Paul Westheim, ed., *Künstlerbekenntnisse*, Berlin, Propyläen Verlag, (n. d.), p. 237.

[8] Karl Ernst Osthaus founded the Folkwang Museum in his native Hagen in 1902 to house principally his own collection of impressionist and post-impressionist paintings. This early museum of modern art was designed by his friend, Henry van de Velde. In 1922, after his death, the Folkwang Museum was transferred to the city of Essen, and a handsome new building was built after World War II. The city of Hagen now has its own museum, which is called Karl-Ernst-Osthaus-Museum in memory of the great collector.

[9] Karl Schmidt-Rottluff in Nolde, *Jahre der Kämpfe*, pp. 90-91.

[10] Nolde, *Jahre der Kämpfe*, p. 91.

[11] Nolde in Fehr, *op. cit.*, p. 53.

[12] Nolde, *Jahre der Kämpfe*, p. 95.

[13] Nolde in Fehr, *op. cit.*, p. 63.

[14] Nolde, *Jahre der Kämpfe*, p. 104.

[15] *Ibid.*, p. 107.

[16] Nolde never wanted to part with this nine-part work and retained it in his own collection. It is now permanently installed in the Nolde Museum in Seebüll.

[17] Nolde, *Jahre der Kämpfe*, p. 189.

[18] (Karl) With, "Künstlerbrief Lübeck," *Feuer*, vol. III, no. 2-3 (Nov.-Dec. 1921), pp. 15-18.

[19] For a more detailed history of the *Berliner Sezession* and the *Neue Sezession* see Selz, *German Expressionist Painting*, Berkeley and Los Angeles, University of California Press, 1957, pp. 36-38, 113-114.

[20] The German expressionists were not alone in their conviction that they had assumed the succession of the School of Paris. The futurists in Italy announced the same thing at the same time. More than a generation later a similar belief prevailed among members of the New York School.

[21] Nolde, *Jahre der Kämpfe*, p. 196.

[22] Nolde's *Welt und Heimat*, which is the third volume of his autobiography, has not yet been published, but will appear shortly at the Christian Wolff Verlag, Flensburg. It deals with Nolde's trip to the South Seas and his activities in Germany during World War I.

[23] Nolde, letter to Hans Fehr, May 24, 1914, in Fehr, *op. cit.*, pp. 86-88.

[24] Nolde, *Jahre der Kämpfe*, p. 182.

[25] *Ibid.*, p. 96.

[26] *Ibid.*, p. 93.

[27] *Ibid.*

[28] Nolde was interested in van Gogh as early as 1898 when he saw van Gogh's *Self Portrait* on exhibition in Munich.

[29] Nolde, introduction to the catalog of his exhibition at the Kunstverein, Cologne, 1950, p. 4.

[30] See Bibl., 86, also 21, 22.

[31] E. L. Kirchner, *Chronik der Brücke*, translated in Selz, *op. cit.*, Appendix A, p. 320.

[32] Nolde, letter to Hans Fehr, Hilchenbach, October 23, 1905, in Westheim, *op. cit.*, p. 234.

[33] Nolde, *Jahre der Kämpfe*, p. 228.

[34] William S. Lieberman in Andrew C. Ritchie, ed., *German Art of the Twentieth Century*, New York, Museum of Modern Art, 1957, p. 200.

[35] Nolde, *Jahre der Kämpfe*, pp. 181-182.

[36] *Ibid.*, p. 183.

[37] Nolde, *Das eigene Leben*, second enlarged edition, Christian Wolff Verlag, Flensburg, 1949, pp. 141-142.

[38] Nolde, *Jahre der Kämpfe*, pp. 88-89.

[39] Nolde in Fehr, *op. cit.*, p. 65.

[40] Verfügung des Präsidenten der Reichskammer der bildenden Kunst, August 23, 1941, quoted in Fehr, *op. cit.*, p. 154.

[41] Paul Klee, in *Festschrift für Emil Nolde*, Dresden, Neue Kunst Fides, 1927, p. 25.

BIOGRAPHICAL CHRONOLOGY

1867 August 7, born as Emil Hansen on a farm in North Schleswig near Nolde.

1884-88 Flensburg. Apprentice at Sauermann's furniture factory.

1888-89 Munich and Karlsruhe. Works in furniture factories as journeyman; part-time art student in Karlsruhe.

1889-91 Berlin.

1892-98 St. Gall, Switzerland. Teacher at Museum for Industrial Arts.

1896 Completes his first oil painting: *Mountain Giants.*

1898 Munich. Studies with Friedrich Fehr. First etchings.

1899 Munich. Studies with Adolf Hölzel. Travels to Paris in the autumn.

1900 Paris. Student at Académie Julian; frequent visits to Louvre: is particularly impressed by paintings of Titian, Rembrandt and Goya. Moves to Copenhagen in the autumn.

1901 Copenhagen. Meets Ada Vilstrup.

1902 Berlin. Marries Ada Vilstrup; changes name to Emil Nolde.

1903 Flensburg. Summers on the island of Alsen (until 1916).

1904-05 Flensburg, Alsen, and trip to Sicily.

1905 Nolde's first one-man show at Galerie Ernst Arnold, Dresden. Exhibits at Berlin Secession.

1906 Joins *Brücke.* Meets Gustav Schiefler, who introduces him to Edvard Munch. First woodcuts.

1907 Dresden, Alsen, Soest. First lithographs. Schiefler publishes first important critical essay on Emil Nolde (Bibl. 86). Nolde resigns from *Brücke.*

1908 Soest, Jena, Alsen, Copenhagen, Stockholm.

1909 First important religious pictures, including *The Last Supper* and *Pentecost.*

1910 Hamburg and Berlin. Paintings, drawings and prints of Hamburg harbor. Nolde's entries rejected by Berlin Secession; he is co-founder of the *Neue Sezession* and participates in its exhibition.

1911 Nolde expelled from Berlin Secession. Visits Ensor in Ostend. Important exhibition at Galerie Commeter, Hamburg. Publication of first volume of definitive catalog of Nolde's prints (Bibl. 21).

1912 Participates in second *Blaue Reiter* exhibition in Munich and *Sonderbund* exhibition in Cologne. Meets futurists in Berlin.

1913 Great series of color lithographs. In the autumn sets out on expedition to the South Seas.

1914 Returns from Melanesia and Asia to Berlin and Alsen.

1915 Paints *The Entombment.*

1916 Moves his summer residence from the island of Alsen to Utenwarf on the mainland. Remains in Berlin during the winters until 1940. Exhibition at J. B. Neumann, Berlin.

1917-22 One-man shows in Frankfurt, Hanover, Munich, Dresden, Hamburg, Wiesbaden, Kiel, Essen, Lübeck, Berlin.

1921 Trip to England, France, Spain. Max Sauerlandt's monograph is published (Bibl. 20).

1925 Trip to Italy.

1926 Buys farm in Seebüll and moves his summer residence there. Honorary doctorate, University of Kiel.

1927 Large retrospective exhibition on the occasion of his sixtieth birthday: Dresden, Hamburg, Kiel, Essen, Wiesbaden. *Festschrift für Emil Nolde* (Bibl. 14). Publication of second volume of the catalog of his graphic works (Bibl. 22).

1928 Large exhibition at Kunsthalle, Basel.

1931 Appointed member of Prussian Academy of Fine Arts. Included in exhibition, *German Painting and Sculpture,* Museum of Modern Art, New York. Publication of first volume of his autobiography (Bibl. 3).

1934 Publication of second volume of his autobiography (Bibl. 4).

1935 Successful operation for cancer.

1937 Nolde's works are shown at Nazi Degenerate Art exhibition in Munich and other German cities; his pictures and prints are removed from German museums and confiscated by the German government.

1939 First one-man show in U. S. at Curt Valentin's Buchholz Gallery, New York.

1940 One-man show at the Katharine Kuh Gallery, Chicago.

1941 Forbidden to exhibit, sell or paint by the Nazi government.

1942 Travels to Vienna to appeal, unsuccessfully, for clemency from Nazi persecution.

1943 Berlin studio, containing most of his graphic work, destroyed by Allied bombing.

1946 First postwar exhibition in Hamburg. Appointed professor by government of Schleswig-Holstein. Death of Ada.

1947 Eightieth birthday celebration. Exhibitions in Berlin, Hamburg, Kiel and Lübeck.

1948 Marriage to Jolanthe Erdmann. Trip to Switzerland. Important retrospective exhibition at Kestner-Gesellschaft, Hanover.

1952 XXVI Venice Biennale. Prize for graphic work. 85th birthday celebration in Seebüll. Retrospective exhibition in Kiel and Mannheim.

1956 April 13. Nolde's death in Seebüll. Creation of Nolde Foundation.

1957 Opening of Nolde Museum in Seebüll. Large memorial exhibition (550 works) at Hamburg Kunstverein.

SELECTED BIBLIOGRAPHY

By Inga Forslund, *Reference Librarian,*
The Museum of Modern Art

TEXTS BY NOLDE *(arranged chronologically)*

1. Aus Leben und Werkstatt Emil Noldes. Auszüge aus Briefen Emil Noldes, zusammengestellt und erläutert von Hans Fehr. *In* Westheim, Paul, Künstlerbekenntnisse: Briefe, Tagebuch-blätter, Betrachtungen heutiger Künstler. Gesammelt und her-ausgegeben von Paul Westheim. Berlin, Propyläen, [1925]. p. 233-239.

2. Briefe aus den Jahren 1894-1926. Herausgegeben und mit einem Vorwort versehen von Max Sauerlandt. Berlin, Furche, [1927]. 183p. port.

3. Das eigene Leben. Berlin, Rembrandt, 1931. 204p. incl. ill.
    2d ed., Flensburg, Christian Wolff, 1949. First volume of autobiography.

4. Jahre der Kämpfe. Berlin, Rembrandt, 1934. 262p. incl. 16 pl., front.
    2d enl. ed., Flensburg, Christian Wolff, [1958]. Herausge-geben von der Stiftung Seebüll Ada und Emil Nolde. — Also Danish ed.: "En Kunstners Kampår," Copenhagen, Gad, 1958. — Second volume of autobiography, 1902-1914.

5. [Introduction to:] Emil Nolde: Gemälde und Aquarelle, Co-logne, Kunstverein, May 13-July 2, 1950. See also bibl. 101.

6. Emil Nolde zum fünfundachtzigsten Geburtstag. Gedanken und Aussprüche des Malers. *Die Kunst und das schöne Heim* v. 51 no. 1:14 Oct. 1952.

7. Emil Nolde über die Expressionisten. *In* Wingler, Hans Maria, Wie sie einander sahen. Moderne Maler im Urteil ihrer Gefähr-ten. Munich, Langen & Müller, 1957. p. 48.

8. Gedanken und Aufzeichnungen aus Briefen und Lebensbüchern von Emil Nolde. *In* Emil Nolde. Aquarelle. Lübeck, Overbeck-Gesellschaft, June 26-Aug. 14, 1960. See also bibl. 109.

9. Welt und Heimat. Flensburg, Christian Wolff, in publication. Third volume of autobiography, 1914-1919.

10. Reisen - Ächtung - Befreiung, 1919-1946.
    Fourth volume of autobiography. Manuscript to be published.

BOOKS ON NOLDE

11. BAUMGART, FRITZ. Emil Nolde. Ein Gedenkbüchlein. Rudol-stadt, 1946.

12. BUSCH, GÜNTER. Emil Nolde. Aquarelle. Nachwort von Gün-ter Busch. Herausgegeben von der Stiftung Seebüll Ada und Emil Nolde. Munich, Piper, c.1957. [51] p. incl. 16 col. pl.

13. FEHR, HANS. Emil Nolde. Ein Buch der Freundschaft. Cologne, DuMont Schauberg, 1957. 182p. incl. ill. col. mount. pl., ports, facsim.

Foreword by Rudolf Probst. — Contains excerpts from let-ters and other writings by Nolde. — Statements by Nolde on Kirchner, p. 151-152.

14. Festschrift für Emil Nolde anlässlich seines 60. Geburtstages. Dresden, Neue Kunst Fides, 1927. 42p. plus [38] pl.
    Contains contributions by Paul Klee and others. — Intro-duction by Rudolf Probst.

15. GOSEBRUCH, MARTIN. Nolde. Aquarelle und Zeichnungen. Ein-führung von Martin Gosebruch. Herausgegeben von der Stif-tung Seebüll Ada und Emil Nolde. Munich, Bruckmann, c.1957. 74p. incl. 21 pl. (mostly col.)

16. HAFTMANN, WERNER. Emil Nolde. N. Y., Abrams, 1959. [92] p. incl. ill. plus 46 col.pl. — Includes bibliography.
    Translated by Norbert Guterman from the German edition, DuMont Schauberg, Cologne, 1958.

17. HOFFMANN, RUDOLF, ed. Holzschnitte von Emil Nolde. Zwan-zig Wiedergaben. Herausgegeben von Rudolf Hoffmann mit Einleitung von Werner Haftmann. Bremen, Hertz, 1947. [8]p. plus 20 pl.

18. HOFFMANN, RUDOLF, ed. Radierungen von Emil Nolde. Vier-zig Wiedergaben. Herausgegeben von Rudolf Hoffmann mit Einleitung von Werner Haftmann. Bremen, Hertz, 1948. [5] p. plus 40 plates.

19. NOLDE, ADA UND EMIL, STIFTUNG, SEEBÜLL. Jahrbuch. Flens-burg, Christian Wolff. 1957/58 — [1961].
    a) *1957/58:* Festschrift. Ausstellungseröffnung am 25. April 1957 im Hause Seebüll. Ada und Emil Nolde zum Ge-dächtnis. Zusammenstellung und Nachwort: Joachim v. Lepel. 50p. plus ill. Includes bibliography.
    b) *1958/59:* Jahrbuch . . . Max Sauerlandt zum Gedächtnis. 53p. plus ill. Includes bibliography. See also bibl. 20.
    c) *1961:* Seebüll III. Emil Nolde von Max Sauerlandt. Aus den Vorlesungen über die Kunst der letzten 30 Jahre, Hamburg 1933. [See also bibl. 85.] — Die "ungemalten Bilder" von Joachim v. Lepel. 109p. plus ill. Includes bibliography.

20. SAUERLANDT, MAX. Emil Nolde. Munich, Curt Wolff, 1921. 85p. plus 100 pl. (some mount. col.)
    A slightly abridged edition was published in Jahrbuch der Stiftung Seebüll Ada und Emil Nolde 1958/59.

21. SCHIEFLER, GUSTAV. Das graphische Werk Emil Noldes bis 1910. Berlin, Julius Bard, 1911. 139p. incl. ill.

22. SCHIEFLER, GUSTAV. Das graphische Werk von Emil Nolde 1910-1925. Berlin, Euphorion, [1927]. 172p. incl. ill.

23. SCHMIDT, PAUL-FERDINAND. Emil Nolde. Berlin, Klinkhardt & Biermann, 1929. 16p. plus 32 pl., col.front. (Junge Kunst. Bd. 53.)

24. URBAN, MARTIN. Emil Nolde. Südsee-Skizzen. Herausgegeben von der Stiftung Seebüll Ada und Emil Nolde. Nachwort von Martin Urban. Munich, Piper, c1961. 57p. incl. ill. (16 col.pl.)
    A selection of his South Sea sketches in their original size.

GENERAL WORKS

25. APOLLONIO, UMBRO. "Die Brücke" e la cultura dell'espressionismo. Venice, Alfieri, 1952. passim.

26. BUCHHEIM, LOTHAR-GÜNTHER. Die Künstlergemeinschaft Brücke. Feldafing, Buchheim, c.1956. p. 317-336 and passim. ill. nos. 354-399.

27. ECKARDT, FERDINAND. Berliner Graphiker der Gegenwart. Baden bei Vienna, Graphische Künste, 1931.

28. EINSTEIN, CARL. Die Kunst des 20. Jahrhunderts. 3. Aufl. Berlin, Propyläen, 1931. p. 157-162, 642, ill. p. 441-445 plus col. pl.18.

29. GEROLD, KARL GUSTAV. Deutsche Malerei unserer Zeit. Vienna, Munich, Basel, Verlag Desch, c.1956. p. 53-56 and passim.

30. GROHMANN, WILL. Bildende Kunst und Architektur. Berlin, Suhrkamp, 1953. p. 60-62 and passim ill. pl. 6 (Zwischen den beiden Kriegen. Bd. 3.)

31. HAFTMANN, WERNER. Painting in the twentieth century. N. Y., Praeger, 1960. v.1 (text) p. 83-85 and passim; v.2 (ill.) p. 74-75, 82-85 (1 col.)
   A completely revised version of the German edition published in 1954-1955 and 1957 by Prestel, Munich.

32. HÄNDLER, GERHARD. German painting in our time. Berlin, Rembrandt, 1956. p. 14-15, pl. 20-23 (1 col.)
   Translation of the German edition, 1956.

33. HARTLAUB, GUSTAV FRIEDRICH. Kunst und Religion. Leipzig, Kurt Wolff, 1919. p. 82, 85, 87-88, 89-91, 94-96 ill. pl. 55-63. (Das neue Bild. Hrsg. v. Carl Georg Heise. Bd. 2.)

34. HAUSENSTEIN, WILHELM. Die bildende Kunst der Gegenwart. Malerei, Plastik, Zeichnung. 2. Aufl., Stuttgart and Berlin, Deutsche Verlags-Anstalt, 1920. p. 323-327 and passim.
   1st edition published 1914.

35. HISTORY OF MODERN PAINTING. Geneva, Skira, c.1949-1950. v. 2 Matisse, Munch, Rouault: Fauvism, Expressionism. p. 112-114 incl. ill. and passim.
   Also other language editions. Special bibliography in German edition.

36. JOLLOS, WALDEMAR. Arte tedesca fra le due guerre con un saggio introduttivo e a cura di Luigi Rognoni. Verona, Mondadori, 1955. p. 151-162.

37. JUSTI, LUDWIG. Von Corinth bis Klee. Berlin, Julius Bard, 1931. p. 117-122, pl. 47, 48.

38. KNAUF, ERICH. Empörung und Gestaltung. Künstlerprofile von Daumier bis Kollwitz. Berlin, Buchmeister, 1928. p. 145-154 incl. ill.

39. KÖHN, HEINZ. Neuere Meister der letzten fünfzig Jahre aus dem Museum Folkwang zu Essen. Cologne, Seemann, c1958. p. [5-6] plus 2 col. pl.
   Color reproductions and analysis of "The Burid of Mary of Egypt" and "Nusa lik."

40. KUHN, CHARLES L. German expressionism and abstract art. The Harvard collections. Cambridge, Mass., Harvard University Press, 1957. passim.

41. MYERS, BERNARD S. The German expressionists. A generation in revolt. N. Y., Praeger, 1957. passim.

42. NEMITZ, FRITZ. Deutsche Malerei der Gegenwart. Munich, Piper, 1948. p. 72-75 incl. ill.

43. NEW YORK. MUSEUM OF MODERN ART. German art of the twentieth century. By Werner Haftmann, Alfred Hentzen, William S. Lieberman, edited by Andrew Carnduff Ritchie. N. Y., The Museum, 1957. passim (index p. 239).

44. PLATTE, HANS. Malerei. Munich, Piper, 1957. p. 180-185 incl. 3 ill. (Die Kunst des 20. Jahrhunderts. Hrsg. v. Carl Georg Heise.)

45. RAYNAL, MAURICE. Modern painting. Geneva, Skira, c1953. passim (index p. 331).
   Also other language editions and revisions.

46. READ, HERBERT. Art now. Rev. and enl. ed. London, Faber and Faber, 1948. p. 83-84.

47. SAUERLANDT, MAX. Die Kunst der letzten 30 Jahre. Herausgegeben durch Harald Busch. Berlin, Rembrandt, 1935. p. 73-135.
   Lectures given in 1933, three of them on Nolde. The first lecture is almost identical with the article in the *Zeitschrift für bildende Kunst*, 1914 (bibl. 85). This edition of the book was confiscated and banned by the Nazis soon after it appeared. A new unabridged edition was published in 1948, Verlag Laatzen, Hamburg. A slightly abridged version appears in Emil Nolde, Seebüll III (bibl.19c).

48. SCHIEFLER, GUSTAV. Meine Graphik-Sammlung. Hamburg, Gesellschaft der Bücherfreunde, 1927. p. 40-46 plus 1 pl.

49. SCHMIDT, PAUL FERDINAND. Geschichte der modernen Malerei. 4. Aufl., Stuttgart, Kohlhammer, 1954. p. 164-170 incl. 2 ill. (1 col.) and passim.
   1st ed. 1952. Frequently revised.

50. SELZ, PETER. German expressionist painting. Berkeley and Los Angeles, University of California Press, 1957. p. 120-129 and passim plus ill. pl.

51. VOLBEHR, THEODOR. Führungen im Kaiser-Friedrich-Museum der Stadt Magdeburg. II:Part 14 "Vom Expressionismus (Emil Nolde — Erich Heckel)," Magdeburg n. d. 8p.

52. WESTHEIM, PAUL. Helden und Abenteurer. Welt und Leben der Künstler. Berlin, Reckendorf, c.1930. p. 207-209.

53. WESTHEIM, PAUL. Das Holzschnittbuch. Potsdam, Kiepenheuer, 1921. p. 152 and passim. ill. p. 165-166.

54. WINKLER, WALTER. Psychologie der modernen Kunst. Tübingen, Alma Mater, c.1949. p. 173-184 incl. 3 ill. (1 col. pl.)

ARTICLES ON NOLDE

55. ASHTON, DORE. Nolde: archtype expressionist. *Art Digest* v.28 no.1:15,28 incl. 1 ill. Apr.1,1954.
   Review of exhibition at Borgenicht Gallery.

56. BENNINGHOFF, LUDWIG. Emil Nolde (zu der Ausstellung in Hamburg). *Der Kreis* 4 no.5:263-268 plus 2 ill. May 1927.

57. BENSON, E. M. Emil Nolde. *Parnassus* v.5 no.1:12-14, 25 incl. 2 ill. Jan. 1933.

58. BOYESEN, LARS ROSTRUP. Emil Nolde. *Gutenbergshus, Copenhagen. Årsskrift.* [Copenhagen] 1958. p. [38-51]. col. ill.

59. BRATTSKOVEN, OTTO. Nolde und Matisse, zwei Maler als nationale Repräsentanten. *Der Kreis* 7 no.4:213-216 Apr. 1930

60. BREUNING, MARGARET. [Emil Nolde.] *Arts* v.32 no.1:52 incl. 1 ill. Oct. 1957.
    Review of exhibition of oils and watercolors at the New Gallery, Sept. 25-Oct. 26, 1957.

61. BULLIET, C. J. Around the galleries. *Chicago Daily News* Oct. 5, 1940. (incl. ill.)
    Review of the Nolde exhibition at the Katharine Kuh Gallery. (His first one-man show in Chicago.)

62. FEHR, HANS. Emil Nolde als Lehrer in St. Gallen. *Das Bodenseebuch.* Zürich. 33:46-47, 1947.

63. FLEMMING, HANS THEODOR. Emil Nolde. *Studio* v.155 no. 779: 44-47 incl. ill. (1 col. pl.) Feb. 1958.

64. FLEMMING, HANS THEODOR. Der frühe Nolde. *Die Kunst und das schöne Heim* v.56 no.6:201-205 incl. ill. (1 col.) Mar. 1958.

65. GOLDBERG, I. The last Teuton artist. *Boston Transcript* Apr.29, 1914.

66. GOLDSCHMIDT, LINA. Emil Nolde. *New York Times* May 25, 1930.
    Review of exhibition at the Gallery Ferdinand Moeller.

67. GROHMANN, WILL. Emil Nolde. *Blätter der Galerie Ferdinand Moeller* (Berlin) Feb. 1930:1-16 incl. ill.

68. GURLITT, HILDEBRAND. Zu Emil Noldes Aquarellen. *Die Kunst für alle* 44 no.2:41-42 plus 3 pl. (1 col.) Nov. 1928.

69. HAFTMANN, WERNER. Emil Nolde en het duitse expressionisme. *Museumjournal* s.4 no.1:6-11, ill. p. 17, June 1958.
    On the occasion of the Nolde exhibition at the Stedelijk Museum in Amsterdam.

70. HAFTMANN, WERNER. Die Lithographien Emil Noldes. *In* Jahresring 55/56. Stuttgart, Deutsche Verlags-Anstalt, 1955. p.154-170 plus ill.

71. HANOVER. KESTNER-GESELLSCHAFT. Flugschriften. 1. Hanover, 1918. 20p.
    1. Zur Kunst unserer Zeit. Gedanken anläßlich der Emil-Nolde-Ausstellung. CONTENTS: Paul Erich Küppers: Rede gehalten zur Eröffnung der Nolde-Ausstellung am 6. Januar 1918. — Chr. Spengemann: Stellung zur Kunst. — Wilh. V. Debschitz: Ein Gespräch. — Hans Kaiser: Emil Nolde.

72. HASINGER, HERMANN. Die religiösen Bilder von Emil Nolde. *Die Kunst und das schöne Heim* v.56 no.7:252-255 incl. ill. (1 col.). Apr. 1958.

73. HEILMAIER, HANS. Emil Nolde. Un expressioniste nordique. *I 4 soli* 3 no.2:16-17 incl. 1 ill. Mar.-Apr. 1956.

74. HEILMAIER, HANS. Das graphische Schaffen Emil Noldes. *Die Kunst und das schöne Heim* v.56 no.4:121-125 incl. ill. Jan. 1958.

75. HEISE, CARL GEORG. Emil Nolde. Wesen und Weg seiner religiösen Malerei. *Genius* v.1:18-32 incl. 10 mount. pl. 1919.

76. JÄHNER, [HORST]. Nolde, oder Die Tragödie eines Einzelgängers. *Bildende Kunst* 1956:428-431, ill.

77. KLEE, PAUL. Emil Nolde. Bekenntnis zu seinem Werk. *In* Wingler, Hans Maria, Wie sie einander sahen. Moderne Maler im Urteil ihrer Gefährten. Munich, Langen & Müller, 1957. p.62. See also bibl. 7.

78. KLEE, PAUL. Nolde. Jan. 1927. *Arts* v.30 no.2:15 incl. ill. Nov. 1955.
    Tribute by Paul Klee to his fellow artist, published for the first time in English in connection with exhibition of Nolde and Kirchner, "Die Brücke" artists, Nov. 9, 1955-Jan. 8, 1956 at The Museum of Modern Art, New York.

79. LINFERT, CARL. Entzünden und verbrennen. Eine Betrachtung zu Emil Nolde. *Neue Deutsche Hefte* 85:126-133 Jan.-Feb. 1962.

80. PODESTA, ATTILIO. Emil Nolde e l'espressionismo tedesco. *Emporium* v.116 no. 691-92:29-34 incl. ill. port. July-Aug. 1952.

81. PROBST, RUDOLF. Emil Nolde. *Neue Blätter für Kunst und Dichtung.* 2:207-209, 1920.

82. RUHMER, EBERHARD. Emil Nolde: Berliner Nachtleben. *Die Kunst und das schöne Heim* v.57 no.5:166-169 incl. ill. (1 col.) Feb. 1959.

83. RUMPEL, HEINRICH. Emil Nolde. *Werk* 32 no.3:87-92 incl. 5 ill. Mar. 1945.

84. SAKAZAKI, OTSURO. Nolde. *Mizue* no.645:45-52 incl. ill. (1 col.pl.) Feb. 1959.
    In Japanese.

85. SAUERLANDT, MAX. Emil Nolde. *Zeitschrift für bildende Kunst* n. s. 25 v.49 no.7:181-192 incl. ill. 1914.
    This article is almost identical with the first lecture in Sauerlandt, M., Die Kunst der letzten 30 Jahre. (bibl. 47). A slightly abridged version appears in Seebüll III (bibl. 19c).

86. SCHIEFLER, GUSTAV. Emil Nolde. *Zeitschrift für bildende Kunst* n. s. 19 no.2:25-32 incl. ill. 1907.

87. SCHIFF, GERT. Emil Nolde, 1867-1956. *Werk* 45 no. 12:suppl. 231 incl. 1 ill. Dec. 1958.
    Review of exhibition in Kunsthaus, Zürich, Oct.11-Nov.9, 1958.

88. SCHMIDT, PAUL FERDINAND. Emil Nolde. *Jahrbuch der jungen Kunst* (Leipzig) 1923:110-124 incl. ill.

89. SCHRÖTER, HANS. Einflüsse der alten Kunst in Emil Noldes frühen Werken. *In* Edwin Redslob. Zum 70. Geburtstag. Eine Festgabe. Berlin, Blaschker, 1955. p.321-331 incl. ill.

90. SELZ, PETER. Beckoning color in a world of fantasy. *New York Times Book Review* p.7, Apr.17, 1960.
    Review of W. Haftmann: Emil Nolde.

91. URBAN, MARTIN. Gedanken zur Kunst Emil Noldes. Seine späten Aquarelle. *Kunst in Schleswig-Holstein. Jahrbuch.* 1952: 125-137 incl. 4 ill. col. front.

92. WANKMÜLLER, RIKE. Zur Farbe im Werk von Emil Nolde. *Kunstwerk* 12 no.5/6:27-30 plus 1 ill. (col.) Nov.-Dec. 1958.

93. WEISS, KONRAD. Emil Nolde als Graphiker, ausgestellt im Graphischen Kabinett, München. *Die Kunst für alle* 42:226-232 incl. 6 ill. 1926/27.

94. WINTZEN, RENE. Corinth et Nolde. Deux grands peintres allemands. *Les Beaux Arts* (Brussels) 16 no.553:9 Dec.28, 1951.

95. WYSS, HEDY A. Emil Nolde. *Werk* 36 no.4: Suppl. p. 40-41 Apr. 1949.
    Review of exhibition at the Kupferstichkabinett der ETH, Zurich, Feb.-Apr. 1949.

SELECTED CATALOG (*arranged chronologically*)

96. NEUMANN, J. B., GRAPHISCHES KABINETT, BERLIN. Graphische Ausstellung Emil Nolde. Berlin [1916]. 16p. ill.
    Exhibition March 1916. — 144 works.

97. VIENNA. GESELLSCHAFT ZUR FÖRDERUNG MODERNER KUNST. Ausstellung Emil Nolde. [Vienna, 1924.] 13p.
    Exhibition Mar.11-Apr.8, 1924. — 141 works. — Introduction by Hans Tietze (p.3-7).

98. BASEL. KUNSTHALLE. Ausstellung Emil Nolde. [Basel, 1928.] 16p. plus 8 pl.
    Exhibition Oct.11-Nov.4, 1928. — 169 works. — Introduction by Georg Schmidt (p.1-9).

99. NEW YORK. MUSEUM OF MODERN ART. German painting and sculpture. N. Y., 1931. 43p. plus 48 ill.
    Exhibition March 13-Apr. 26, 1931. — 6 works by Nolde. — Text on Nolde, p.32.

100. HANOVER. KESTNER-GESELLSCHAFT. Emil Nolde. Hanover, 1948. [21]p. incl. ill.
    Exhibition Oct.-Nov. 1948. — 145 works. — Introduction by Alfred Hentzen. — Includes extract from a letter by Nolde.

101. COLOGNE. KUNSTVEREIN. Emil Nolde. Gemälde und Aquarelle. Cologne, 1950. [10]p. plus 9 ill., front.
    Exhibition May 13-July 2, 1950. — 40 works. — Introduction by Nolde p.[4-6]. See also bibl. 5.

102. KIEL. KUNSTHALLE. Emil Nolde. [Kiel, 1952.] 14p. plus 9 pl.
    Exhibition June 22-July 27, 1952. — 208 works. — Contains "Auszüge aus der von Rudolf Probst 1927 herausgegebenen Festschrift zum 60. Geburtstag des Künstlers." — Also facsimile of text by Paul Klee.

103. BREMEN. KUNSTHALLE. Emil Nolde. Das graphische Werk. [Bremen, 1956.] 20p. incl. ill.
    Exhibition of the Bernhard Sprengel collection, Hanover, Feb. 12-Mar. 25, 1956. — 447 works.

104. KIEL. KUNSTHALLE. Emil Nolde. Gedächtnisausstellung. [Kiel, 1956.] [35]p. plus 24 pl.
    Exhibition Dec.9, 1956-Jan.13, 1957. — 209 works. — Introduction by Leonhardi. — Includes short bibliography.

105. HAMBURG. KUNSTVEREIN. Gedächtnisausstellung Emil Nolde. Hamburg, 1957. 40p. plus 210 ill. (pt. col.).
    Exhibition Apr.27-June16, 1957. — 550 works. — Foreword by Alfred Hentzen p.5-21.

106. NEW YORK. MUSEUM OF MODERN ART. German art of the twentieth century. N. Y., 1957. 239p. incl. ill. (pt. col.) Includes bibliography.
    Exhibition Oct.1-Dec.8, 1957. — 11 works by Nolde. See also bibl. 43.

107. HELSINKI. ATENEUM. Emil Nolde. Helsinki, 1958. [36]p. incl. ill. (pt.col.).
    Exhibition Sept.16-Dec.7, 1958. — 107 works. — Introduction by Klaus Leonhardi. — Text in Finnish and Swedish.

108. ZÜRICH. KUNSTHAUS. Emil Nolde. [Zürich, 1958.] 29, [19]p. plus 11 pl. (6 col.)
    Exhibition Oct.11-Nov.9, 1958. — 207 works. — Introduction by Alfred Hentzen (p. 5-19). — Includes extracts from Nolde's autobiography (p. 20-25), biographical notes (p. 26-28), bibliography (p. 29).

109. LÜBECK. OVERBECK-GESELLSCHAFT. Emil Nolde. Aquarelle. [Lübeck, 1960.] [22]p. incl. 7 col. pl., front. (port.).
    Exhibition June 26-Aug. 14, 1960. — 78 works. — Includes: Gedanken und Aufzeichnungen aus Briefen und Lebensbüchern von Emil Nolde.

110. BRUSSELS. PALAIS DES BEAUX-ARTS. Emil Nolde. Brussels, 1961. [22]p. plus 199 ill. (pt.col.).
    Exhibition May-June 1961. — 244 works. — Introduction by Werner Haftmann. — Includes biography. — Text in French.

111. HANOVER. KUNSTVEREIN. Emil Nolde. Ölgemälde — Aquarelle — Zeichnungen. Hanover, 1961. [22]p. plus 68 ill. (pt. col.).
    Exhibition July 16-Sept. 3, 1961. — 177 works. — Introduction by Gert von der Osten. — Text in German.

112. MUNICH. HAUS DER KUNST. Entartete Kunst. Bildersturm vor 25 Jahren. Munich, 1962. xxxii, 432 p. incl. ill. (pt. col.).
    Exhibition Oct. 25-Dec. 16, 1962. — Text by Jürgen Klaus. — In German.

CATALOG

OILS

* 1. *Moonlit Night (Mondnacht).* (1903). Oil on canvas, 25¹/₂ x 32⁵/₈". Signed lower right. Wallraf-Richartz-Museum, Cologne. Ill. p. 12

2. *Summer Guest - Man under Trees (Feriengast - Mann unter Bäumen).* 1904. Oil on canvas, 28³/₄ x 34¹/₄". Signed and dated lower right. Nolde Foundation, Seebüll

* 3. *Spring Indoors (Frühling im Zimmer).* 1904. Oil on canvas, 34⁷/₈ x 28⁷/₈". Signed and dated lower right. Nolde Foundation, Seebüll. Ill. p. 13

* 4. *Harvest Day (Erntetag).* (1904). Oil on canvas, 28³/₄ x 35⁷/₈". Signed lower right. Collection Andreas Kohlschütter-Fehr, Cambridge, Massachusetts. (Exhibited in New York only) Ill. p. 13

* 5. *The Free Spirit (Freigeist).* (1907). Oil on canvas, 27¹/₈ x 35". Signed lower right. Nolde Foundation, Seebüll. Ill. p. 16

6. *Red and Yellow Roses (Rote und gelbe Rosen).* 1907. Oil on canvas, 25³/₈ x 32¹/₂". Signed and dated lower left. Wallraf-Richartz-Museum, Cologne

7. *Cattle in the Lowland (Ochsen im Koog).* 1909. Oil on canvas, 27 x 35". Signed and dated lower right. Los Angeles County Museum of Art. Gift of Josef von Sternberg

8. *The Forest Path (Waldweg).* (1909). Oil on canvas, 35 x 27¹/₈". Signed lower left. Collection Dr. Rauert, Hamburg.

* 9. *The Last Supper (Abendmahl).* 1909. Oil on canvas, 34⁵/₈ x 42¹/₂". Signed and dated lower right. The Royal Museum of Fine Arts, Copenhagen. Ill. p. 18

10. *Man and Little Girl (Mann und kleines Mädchen).* (1910). Oil on canvas, 34⁵/₈ x 26³/₄". Nolde Foundation, Seebüll

* 11. *Dance Around the Golden Calf (Tanz um das goldene Kalb).* (1910). Oil on canvas, 34⁵/₈ x 41⁵/₈". Signed lower left. Nolde Foundation, Seebüll. Ill. p. 21

* 12. *Christ Among the Children (Christus und die Kinder).* (1910). Oil on canvas, 34¹/₂ x 41⁷/₈". Signed lower left. The Museum of Modern Art, New York. Gift of Dr. W. R. Valentiner. Ill. p. 20

13. *Smoking Steamers (Qualmende Dampfer).* (1910). Oil on canvas, 22¹/₂ x 28³/₈". Nolde Foundation, Seebüll

* 14. *A Glass of Wine (Am Weintisch).* (1911). Oil on canvas, 34⁵/₈ x 28³/₄". Signed lower right. Nolde Foundation, Seebüll. Ill. p. 29

* 15. *Slovenes (Slowenen).* (1911). Oil on canvas, 31¹/₂ x 27¹/₄". Signed upper left. Nolde Foundation, Seebüll. Ill. p. 29

* 16. *Still Life of Masks I (Maskenstilleben I).* (1911). Oil on canvas, 28³/₄ x 30¹/₂". Signed lower left. Nelson Gallery of Art. Atkins Museum, Kansas City, Missouri (Friends of Art Collection). (Exhibited in New York and San Francisco only). Ill. p. 30

17. *Woman In Bright Light (Frau in hellem Licht).* (1912). Oil on canvas, 23¹/₂ x 19". Collection Mr. and Mrs. Morton D. May, St. Louis

18. *Mother and Child (Mutter und Kind).* (1912). Oil on canvas, 30¹/₄ x 28". Signed lower right. Städtische Galerie im Landesmuseum Hanover.

19. *Child and Big Bird (Kind und großer Vogel).* (1912). Oil on canvas, 29 x 32¹/₄". Signed lower center. The Royal Museum of Fine Arts, Copenhagen

* 20. *Candle Dancers (Kerzentänzerinnen).* (1912). Oil on canvas, 39³/₈ x 33¹/₂". Signed lower left. Nolde Foundation, Seebüll. Ill. cover and p. 31

* 21. *Mary of Egypt: In the Port of Alexandria (Maria Aegyptiaca: Im Hafen von Alexandrien).* (1912). Oil on canvas, 33⁷/₈ x 39³/₈". Signed lower left. Kunsthalle, Hamburg. Ill. p. 22

* 22. *Mary of Egypt: The Conversion (Maria Aegyptiaca: Die Bekehrung).* (1912). Oil on canvas, 41³/₈ x 47¹/₄". Signed lower left. Kunsthalle, Hamburg. Ill. pp. 22, 23

* 23. *Mary of Egypt: Death in the Desert (Maria Aegyptiaca: Der Tod in der Wüste).* (1912). Oil on canvas, 33⁷/₈ x 39³/₈". Signed lower center. Kunsthalle, Hamburg. Ill. p. 22

24. *Mother and Child (Mutter und Kind).* (1913). Oil on canvas, 27¹/₂ x 21⁷/₈". Signed lower left. Collection Otto Schäfer, Schweinfurt

25. *Battlefield (Schlachtfeld).* (1913). Oil on canvas, 41³/₄ x 47¹/₄". Nolde Foundation, Seebüll

* 26. *The Sea III (Das Meer III).* (1913). Oil on canvas, 34 x 39³/₈". Signed lower left. Nolde Foundation, Seebüll. Ill. p. 39

* 27. *Flower Garden (Blumengarten).* (c. 1913). Oil on canvas, 28³/₄ x 34³/₄". Signed lower right. Collection Mr. and Mrs. Morton D. May, St. Louis. Ill. p. 50

* 28. *Nusa lik.* (1914). Oil on canvas, 27¹/₂ x 41". Signed upper left. Museum Folkwang, Essen. (Exhibited in New York only). Ill. p. 34

* 29. *The Ruler (Der Herrscher).* (1914). Oil on canvas, 34⁵/₈ x 40¹/₈". Signed lower right. Galerie Rudolf Hoffmann, Hamburg. Ill. p. 36

* 30. *The Two Goldsmiths (Goldschmiede).* (c. 1914). Oil on wood, 28 x 20". Signed lower right. Collection Mr. and Mrs. Thomas M. Futter, Westfield, Massachusetts. Ill. p. 2

* 31. *Russian II (Russe II).* (c. 1914). Oil on canvas, 26¹/₂ x 23". Signed lower right. Collection Larry Aldrich, New York. Ill. p. 37

* 32. *Three Russians (Drei Russen).* 1915. Oil on burlap, 28³/₄ x 39¹/₂". Signed and dated upper right. Collection Mr. and Mrs. David Bakalar, Boston. (Exhibited in New York only). Ill. p. 37

33. *Mulatto (Mulattin).* (1915). Oil on canvas, 30¹/₂ x 28³/₄". Signed lower left. Busch-Reisinger Museum, Harvard University, Cambridge, Massachusetts. Anonymous gift in memory of Curt Valentin

34. *Mr. Sch. (Herr Sch.).* (1915). Oil on canvas, 31⁷/₈ x 28³/₈". Signed lower right. Collection C. G. Schiefler, Hamburg

35. *Summer Guests II (Feriengäste II).* (1915). Oil on canvas, 33¹/₂ x 39³/₈". Signed lower left. Collection Mr. and Mrs. Leo M. Rogers, New York

* 36. *Evening Glow - South Pacific (Abendglut - Meer der Südsee).* (1915). Oil on canvas, 34 x 39¹/₄". Signed lower right. Collection Mr. and Mrs. Donald Winston, Los Angeles. Ill. p. 35

* 37. *The Entombment (Grablegung).* (1915). Oil on canvas, 33⁷/₈ x 46". Signed lower right. Nolde Foundation, Seebüll. Ill. p. 25

38. *Flowers (Blumen).* (1915?). Oil on burlap, 26¹/₄ x 33¹/₄". Signed lower left. The Museum of Modern Art, New York. Gift of Mr. and Mrs. Werner E. Josten

39. *Sea II (Meer II).* (1915?). Oil on canvas, 26³/₄ x 35¹/₄". Signed lower right. Collection Dr. Bernhard Sprengel, Hanover

40. *Landscape with Young Horses (Landschaft mit jungen Pferden).* (1916). Oil on canvas, 28³/₄ x 39³/₈". Signed lower right. Nolde Foundation, Seebüll

41. *Fishing Boat (Fischkutter).* (1916). Oil on canvas, 34⁵/₈ x 28³/₄". Signed lower right. Nolde Foundation, Seebüll

42. *Self Portrait (Selbstbild).* (1917). Oil on wood, 32³/₄ x 25⁵/₈". Signed lower right. Nolde Foundation, Seebüll

43. *Polish Girl (Polnisches Mädchen).* (1917). Oil on canvas, 35¹/₂ x 32³/₄". World House Galleries, New York

44. *Brother and Sister (Bruder und Schwester).* (1918). Oil on canvas, 30³/₄ x 25⁵/₈". Signed upper right. Nolde Foundation, Seebüll

45. *Young Girl (Junges Mädchen).* (1918). Oil on canvas, 34¹/₂ x 18¹/₈". Signed upper right. Nolde Foundation, Seebüll

46. *Ingeborg.* (1919). Oil on canvas, 16¹/₄ x 10³/₄". Signed lower left. Collection Herbert Mayer, New York

47. *Dancers (Tänzerinnen).* (1920). Oil on canvas, 41³/₄ x 34⁵/₈". Signed lower left. Staatsgalerie Stuttgart

* 48. *Christ and the Adulteress (Christus und die Sünderin).* (1926). Oil on canvas, 33⁷/₈ x 41³/₄". Signed upper left. Dr. Walther Berndorff, Cologne. Ill. p. 26

* 49. *"Be ye as little children" (So ihr nicht werdet wie die Kinder).* 1929. Oil on canvas, 41³/₄ x 47¹/₄". Signed and dated lower right. Collection Ernst Henke, Essen. (Exhibited in New York only). Ill. p. 27

50. *Sea E (Meer E).* (1930). Oil on wood, 28³/₄ x 39³/₈". Signed lower left. Nolde Foundation, Seebüll

* 51. *Sultry Evening (Schwüler Abend).* (1930). Oil on canvas, 28³/₄ x 39³/₈". Signed lower right. Nolde Foundation, Seebüll. Ill. p. 43

52. *The Family (Die Familie).* (1931). Oil on canvas, 39³/₈ x 28¹/₂". Signed lower right. Nolde Foundation, Seebüll

* 53. *Ripe Sunflowers (Reife Sonnenblumen).* (1932). Oil on canvas, 29 x 35". Signed lower center. The Detroit Institute of Arts. Ill. p 46

54. *In the Lemon Grove (Im Zitronengarten).* (1933). Oil on canvas, 28³/₄ x 35". Signed lower right. Collection Dr.-Ing. E. H. Max Lütze, Bad Homburg vor der Höhe

* 55. *Frisian Farm on a Canal (Friesengehöft am Kanal).* (1935). Oil on canvas, 28³/₄ x 34⁵/₈". Signed lower right. Nolde Foundation, Seebüll. Ill. p. 48

56. *Flowers and Clouds (Blumen und Wolken).* (1938). Oil on canvas, 28³/₄ x 34⁵/₈". Collection Dr. Bernhard Sprengel, Hanover

* 57. *The Great Gardener (Der große Gärtner).* (1940). Oil on canvas, 27¹/₂ x 22". Signed lower right. Collection Dr. Bernhard Sprengel, Hanover. Ill. p. 45

* 58. *Great Poppies - Red, Red, Red (Großer Mohn - Rot, rot, rot).* (1942). Oil on canvas, 28³/₄ x 34¹/₂". Signed lower right. Nolde Foundation, Seebüll. Ill. p. 47

59. *Sunflowers in the Storm (Sonnenblumen im Sturmwind).* (1943). Oil on wood, 28³/₄ x 34⁵/₈". Signed lower right. Nolde Foundation, Seebüll

60. *Two Figures (Zwei Menschen).* 1945. Oil on wood, 34⁵/₈ x 26³/₈". Signed and dated lower right. Nolde Foundation, Seebüll

61. *Friends (Freundinnen).* (1946). Oil on canvas, 27¹/₂ x 22". Signed lower right. Nolde Foundation, Seebüll

* 62. *Luminous Sea (Lichtes Meer).* (1948). Oil on canvas, 26³/₄ x 34⁵/₈". Signed lower left. Nolde Foundation, Seebüll. Ill. p. 40

WATERCOLORS AND DRAWINGS

Early Landscapes and Portraits

63. *Before Sunrise.* (1894). Watercolor, 3¹/₄ x 4". Nolde Foundation, Seebüll. Ill. p. 61

* 64. *Sunset.* 1908. Watercolor, 14¹/₄ x 19¹/₄". Signed and dated lower left. Nolde Foundation, Seebüll. Ill. p. 61

65. *Portrait of Maxim Gorky.* 1905. Black chalk, 11⁷/₈ x 8¹/₂". Signed and dated lower right. Kunsthalle, Hamburg

Studies for Religious Pictures 1909

* 66. *Head of an Apostle.* Watercolor, 13³/₄ x 11¹/₄". Signed lower right. Kunsthalle, Hamburg. Ill. p. 64

67. *Head of a Prophet.* Watercolor, 15³/₄ x 12³/₄". City Art Museum of St. Louis

Hamburg Harbor 1910

68. *Pier in Hamburg Harbor.* India ink, 9⁷/₈ x 12¹/₄". Signed lower right. Kunsthalle, Hamburg

* 69. *Steamer on the Elbe.* Pen and wash, 13¹/₈ x 9⁷/₈". Signed lower left and lower right. Wallraf-Richartz-Museum, Cologne. Ill. p. 62

70. *Tugboat.* India ink on Japan paper, 9¹/₈ x 13³/₈". Signed lower right. Nolde Foundation, Seebüll

71. *Sailboat.* India ink on Japan paper, 13 x 18". Signed and dated lower right. Nolde Foundation, Seebüll

Actors, Dancers and Night Life

72. *Tilla Durieux.* 1907. Watercolor, 18³/₄ x 13³/₄". Signed and dated lower right. Collection Mrs. Heinz Schultz, Great Neck, New York

73. *Three Seated Figures.* (c. 1911). Brush, ink and wash, 8¹/₂ x 12¹/₂". Signed lower right. The Museum of Modern Art, New York. Gift of Curt Valentin

74. *Toe Dancer.* (c. 1911). India ink on Japan paper, 10³/₈ x 11". Signed lower right. Nolde Foundation, Seebüll

75. *Toe Dancer.* (c. 1911). Watercolor, 10³/₈ x 9". Signed lower right. Nolde Foundation, Seebüll

* 76. *Singer.* (c. 1911). Watercolor, 12¹/₂ x 8³/₄". Signed lower right. Kunsthalle, Hamburg. Ill. p. 68

77. *Singer.* (c. 1911). Watercolor, 9 x 6¹/₈". Signed lower right. Kunsthalle, Hamburg

* 78. *Master of Ceremonies.* (c. 1911). India ink on Japan paper, 11¹/₂ x 15". Signed lower right. Nolde Foundation, Seebüll. Ill. p. 28

79. *Two Ladies.* (c. 1911). India ink on Japan paper, 13 x 8⁵/₈". Signed lower right. Nolde Foundation, Seebüll

* 80. *Portrait of Mary Wigman.* (c. 1920). Watercolor, 19 x 15". Signed lower right. Collection Mr. and Mrs. Joseph M. Edinburg, Chestnut Hill, Massachusetts. Ill. p. 65

South Pacific 1913-1914

* 81. *South-Sea Island Chief.* Watercolor, 19 x 13⁵/₈". Signed lower right. Collection Dr. G. Thiem, Hanover. Ill. p. 64

82. *Native - Red Hair.* Watercolor, 20 x 15¹/₈". Signed lower right. Nolde Foundation, Seebüll

83. *Head of a Native.* Watercolor, 19¹/₂ x 15". Signed lower right. Collection Herbert Mayer, New York

* 84. *Chinese Junk.* Watercolor, 10³/₄ x 12¹/₂". Signed upper right. Collection Mr. and Mrs. Eugene Victor Thaw, New York. Ill. p. 62

85. *Chinese Junks.* Watercolor, 9¹/₂ x 11". Signed lower left. Wallraf-Richartz-Museum, Cologne

Figure Studies

Heads

* 86. *Self Portrait.* Watercolor, 18¹/₂ x 13⁷/₈". Signed lower right. Nolde Foundation, Seebüll. Ill. p. 65

87. *Spanish Woman.* (1914). Watercolor, 16 x 12⁵/₈". Signed lower right. Wallraf-Richartz-Museum, Cologne

88. *Spanish Woman.* Watercolor, 18³/₄ x 13¹/₂". Collection Mr. and Mrs. William D. Vogel, Milwaukee

89. *Woman with Red Hair.* (c. 1920). Watercolor, 18¹/₂ x 13¹/₂". Signed lower left. Busch-Reisinger Museum, Havard University. Cambridge, Massachusetts. Gift of Edward M. M. Warburg

90. *Woman.* Watercolor, 18¹/₂ x 13³/₈". Signed lower right. Kunsthalle, Hamburg

91. *Young Girl.* Watercolor, 18¹/₂ x 13⁷/₈". Signed lower right. Nolde Foundation, Seebüll

92. *Portrait of a Boy.* Watercolor, 18 x 13¹/₄". Collection Dr. Henry M. Roland, Woking, Surrey, England

93. *Girl's Head.* Watercolor, 12 x 15". Signed lower right. Collection Henry B. Blunden, Haslemere, Surrey, England

Couples

* 94. *The Lovers (Self Portrait of the Artist with his Wife).* (1932). Watercolor, 13¹/₂ x 19¹/₂". Signed lower center. Collection Mrs. Ala Story, Santa Barbara. Ill. p. 69

95. *The Couple.* (1934). Watercolor, 9¹/₂ x 13". Signed lower right. Collection Alfred and Anne Hentzen, Hamburg

96. *Two Bearded Men.* Watercolor, 16⁵/₈ x 14¹/₄". Signed lower left. Collection Mr. and Mrs. Harry Lynde Bradley, Milwaukee

97. *Magicians.* (1930-34). Watercolor, 20¹/₈ x 14³/₈". Signed lower left. The Museum of Modern Art, New York. Purchase

98. *The Couple.* Watercolor, 17³/₄ x 13¹/₄". Signed lower right. Collection Mr. and Mrs. Max Wilk, Ridgefield, Connecticut

99. *The Couple.* Watercolor, 13¹/₂ x 18". Signed lower right. Collection Mr. and Mrs. C. Bagley Wright, Jr., Seattle

Fantasies

100. *Star Walker.* Watercolor, 17¹/₂ x 11⁷/₈". Signed lower right. Nolde Foundation, Seebüll

101. *Suffragettes.* Watercolor, 21 x 19⁷/₈". Signed lower right. Nolde Foundation, Seebüll

102. *Youth.* Watercolor, 20⁷/₈ x 14³/₈". Signed lower right. Nolde Foundation, Seebüll

Animals

103. *Two Goldfish.* Watercolor, 13¹/₂ x 18³/₈". Signed lower right. Kunsthalle, Hamburg

104. *Flamingos.* Watercolor, 18¹/₂ x 13". Signed lower right. Nolde Foundation, Seebüll

Flowers

105. *Amaryllis and Anemone.* Watercolor, 13³/₄ x 13³/₈". Signed lower right. The Museum of Modern Art, New York. Gift of Philip L. Goodwin

106. *White and Red Amaryllis.* Watercolor, 9¹/₄ x 18". Signed upper left. Kunsthalle, Hamburg

107. *Poppies and Larkspur.* Watercolor, 13¹/₂ x 18". Signed lower right. Collection Mr. and Mrs. Harry Lynde Bradley, Milwaukee

* 108. *Red Poppies.* Watercolor, 13 x 18". Signed lower left. Collection Mr. and Mrs. Hans Popper, San Francisco. Ill. p. 66

109. *Yellow Iris and White Peonies.* Watercolor, 13 x 18". Signed lower right. Collection Mr. and Mrs. Hans Popper, San Francisco

110. *Flowers.* Watercolor, 13¹/₈ x 18¹/₂". Signed lower left. Collection Herbert Mayer, New York

111. *Blue Iris.* Watercolor, 19 x 14". Signed upper right. Collection Mrs. Bliss Parkinson, New York

112. *Dahlias.* Watercolor, 18¹/₂ x 13⁵/₈". Signed lower right. Collection Mr. and Mrs. Harry Lynde Bradley, Milwaukee

113. *Red and Yellow Sunflowers.* Watercolor, 13¹/₄ x 17⁷/₈". Signed lower right. Collection Mr. and Mrs. Harry Lynde Bradley, Milwaukee

114. *Sunflower in Full Bloom.* Watercolor, 13³/₈ x 10⁷/₈". Signed lower right. Nolde Foundation, Seebüll

Landscapes and Seascapes

* 115. *Kurland.* Watercolor, 13³/₈ x 18⁵/₈". Signed lower left. Städtische Galerie im Landesmuseum, Hanover. Ill. p. 63

116. *Northern Seacoast.* Watercolor, 13³/₄ x 18¹/₂". Signed lower right. Wallraf-Richartz-Museum, Cologne

117. *Hills.* Watercolor, 9 x 10³/₄". Signed lower left. Private Collection

118. *The Red Cloud.* Watercolor, 13¹/₂ x 17¹/₄". Signed lower right. Collection Dr. and Mrs. Max M. Stern, New York

119. *Farm by the Wharf.* Watercolor, 13³/₄ x 18³/₄". Signed lower left. Collection Dr. and Mrs. Max M. Stern, New York

120. *Red Evening Clouds.* Watercolor, 13 x 18⁷/₈". Signed lower right. Collection Dr. Bernhard Sprengel, Hanover

121. *Sunset on the Sea.* Watercolor, 13³/₈ x 18¹/₂". Signed lower left. Wallraf-Richartz-Museum, Cologne

122. *Dark Cloud over the Sea.* (c. 1930). Watercolor, 13¹/₂ x 17⁷/₈". Busch-Reisinger Museum, Harvard University Cambridge, Massachusetts. Gift of Sally J. Kuhn. (Exhibited in New York only)

123. *Play of Lights on Lake Zurich.* Watercolor, 13³/₄ x 18³/₈". Signed lower right. Wallraf-Richartz-Museum, Cologne

124. *Evening Sky over Lake Geneva.* Watercolor, 13¹/₄ x 17³/₄". Signed lower right. Nolde Foundation, Seebüll

125. *Mountain Peaks.* Watercolor, 13⁵/₈ x 18¹/₈". Signed lower right. Nolde Foundation, Seebüll

126. *Winter Evening.* Watercolor, 14 x 18¹/₈". Signed lower right. Nolde Foundation, Seebüll

127. *The End of Summer.* Watercolor, 13⁵/₈ x 17⁷/₈". Signed lower right. Nolde Foundation, Seebüll

* 128. *North Sea.* Watercolor, 13¹/₄ x 17⁷/₈". Signed lower right. Nolde Foundation, Seebüll. Ill. p. 63

Unpainted Pictures

* 129. *The Passer-by.* Watercolor and gouache on Japan paper, 9³/₄ x 6⁵/₈". Signed lower left. Nolde Foundation, Seebüll. Ill. p. 75

130. *The Promenade.* Watercolor and gouache on Japan paper, 6¹/₄ x 6³/₄". Signed lower right. Nolde Foundation, Seebüll

131. *Couple Walking.* Watercolor and gouache on Japan paper, 9¹/₈ x 5⁵/₈". Signed lower right. Nolde Foundation, Seebüll

132. *The Skater.* Watercolor and gouache on Japan paper, 9⁷/₈ x 7". Nolde Foundation, Seebüll

133. *Girl in Field of Flowers.* Watercolor and gouache on Japan paper, 9³/₈ x 7". Signed lower right. Nolde Foundation, Seebüll

134. *Two Women in Landscape.* Watercolor and gouache on Japan paper, 8⁷/₈ x 7¹/₈". Signed left side center. Nolde Foundation Seebüll

* 135. *Girls from Far Away.* Watercolor and gouache on Japan paper, 6³/₄ x 10³/₄". Signed lower right. Nolde Foundation, Seebüll. Ill. p. 74

* 136. *Circus People.* Watercolor and gouache on Japan paper, 8³/₈ x 7⁵/₈". Signed lower right. Nolde Foundation, Seebüll. Ill. p. 73

137. *The Silent One.* Watercolor and gouache on Japan paper. 10 x 7¹/₄". Signed bottom left of center. Nolde Foundation, Seebüll

138. *Affection.* Watercolor and gouache on Japan paper, 10 x 7³/₈". Signed upper right. Nolde Foundation, Seebüll

139. *The Pardon.* Watercolor and gouache on Japan paper, 10³/₄ x 9". Signed lower right. Nolde Foundation, Seebüll

140. *Delirium.* Watercolor and gouache on Japan paper, 6³/₄ x 7¹/₈". Nolde Foundation, Seebüll

141. *Consolation.* Watercolor and gouache on Japan paper, 7¹/₈ x 6¹/₂". Signed lower left. Nolde Foundation, Seebüll

142. *Judge and Young Woman.* Watercolor and gouache on Japan paper, 10¹/₈ x 8⁵/₈". Signed lower right. Nolde Foundation, Seebüll

143. *The Love of Flowers.* Watercolor and gouache on Japan paper, 9³/₄ x 6". Signed upper right. Nolde Foundation, Seebüll

144. *Bold Girls.* Watercolor and gouache on Japan paper, 8³/₈ x 5⁵/₈". Nolde Foundation, Seebüll

145. *In the Loge.* Watercolor and gouache on Japan paper, 8⁷/₈ x 5³/₄". Signed lower right. Nolde Foundation, Seebüll

* 146. *Old Man with Beard.* Watercolor and gouache on Japan paper, 10¹/₂ x 9". Signed lower right. Nolde Foundation, Seebüll. Ill. p. 71

147. *Head of a Woman.* Watercolor and gouache on Japan paper, 11³/₈ x 8¹/₄". Signed lower right. Nolde Foundation, Seebüll

* 148. *Little Faun.* Watercolor and gouache on Japan paper, 9 x 5⁵/₈". Signed lower left. Nolde Foundation, Seebüll. Ill. p. 73

149. *Two Sailboats at Dusk.* Watercolor and gouache on Japan paper, 6⁷/₈ x 10⁷/₈". Signed lower right. Nolde Foundation, Seebüll

150. *Rough Sea.* Watercolor and gouache on Japan paper, 7 x 9". Signed upper left. Nolde Foundation, Seebüll

151. *Mountain Landscape.* Watercolor and gouache on Japan paper, 8⁵/₈ x 6". Signed lower right. Nolde Foundation, Seebüll

* 152. *Bird Over Mountains.* Watercolor and gouache on Japan paper, 9 x 6". Signed lower left. Nolde Foundation, Seebüll. Ill. p. 73

153. *Ragamuffins (Lumpen)*. 1898. Drypoint, 3¹³/₁₆ x 2¹/₂″. Signed lower right in pencil. (Sch. R 1, III/III). The Museum of Modern Art, New York. Purchase

154. *Farewell (Abschied)*. (1906). Etching and aquatint, 6³/₄ x 4⁷/₈″. Signed lower right in pencil. (Sch. R 20). Nolde Foundation, Seebüll

155. *Woman's Head (Frauenkopf)*. (1906). Etching, 7⁷/₈ x 6³/₁₆″. (Sch. R 24, V, b). Nolde Foundation, Seebüll

* 156. *Nude (Akt)*. (1906). Etching, 7¹¹/₁₆ x 5⁵/₈″. (Sch. R 34, II, a). Nolde Foundation, Seebüll. Ill. p. 52

157. *Portrait of a Woman (Frauenprofil)*. (1907). Drypoint, 11⁷/₈ x 8³/₄″. Signed lower right in pencil. (Sch. R 68). The Museum of Modern Art, New York. Larry Aldrich Fund

158. *Hugo del Caril*. (1908). Aquatint and etching, 12 x 9⁵/₁₆″. Signed lower right in pencil. (Sch. R 88, II/II). The Museum of Modern Art, New York. Purchase

159. *Self Portrait (Selbstporträt)*. (1908). Etching 12 x 9⁷/₁₆″. (Sch. R 89, II). Nolde Foundation, Seebüll

* 160. *Reclining Woman (Liegendes Weib)*. 1908. Etching and aquatint, printed in green, 12¹/₈ x 18⁵/₈″. Signed lower right in pencil. Sch. R 92, III/III. The Museum of Modern Art, New York. Purchase. Ill. p. 52

161. *Dance I (Tanz I)*. (1908). Etching, 8⁵/₈ x 10³/₈″. (Sch. R 106, III). Nolde Foundation, Seebüll

162. *Dance II (Tanz II)*. (1908.) Etching, 8⁵/₈ x 10³/₈″. (Sch. R 110 III). Nolde Foundation, Seebüll

163. *Street Urchin (Strassenjunge)*. (1908). Etching, 10³/₁₆ x 8¹/₂″. Signed lower right in pencil. (Sch. R 122). The Museum of Modern Art, New York. Purchase

164. *Steamboat (Dampfer)*. (1910). Etching, 12 x 15¹⁵/₁₆″. (Sch. R 135, IV). Nolde Foundation, Seebüll

* 165. *Hamburg Harbor (Hamburg, Freihafen)*. (1910). Etching and aquatint, 12¹/₁₆ x 16¹/₈″. Signed and dated lower right in pencil. (Sch. R 137). Collection Mr. and Mrs. E. Powis Jones, New York. Ill. p. 54

166. *Loading Dock, Hamburg (Reiherstiegdock, Hamburg)*. (1910). Etching, aquatint and drypoint, 12¹/₄ x 16³/₁₆″. Signed lower right in pencil. (Sch. R 145, II/II). The Museum of Modern Art, New York. Gift of Mrs. John D. Rockefeller, Jr.

167. *Solomon and His Wives (Salomo und seine Frauen)*. (1911). Etching and aquatint, 11⁷/₈ x 11⁹/₁₆″. Signed lower right in pencil. (Sch. R 153, II/II). The Museum of Modern Art, New York. Purchase

* 168. *Scribes (Schriftgelehrte)*. (1911). Etching and aquatint, printed in brown-black, 10¹/₂ x 11³/₄″. Signed lower right in pencil. (Sch. R 154, II/II). The Museum of Modern Art, New York. Purchase. Ill. p. 55

* 169. *The Artist's Wife (Frau N.)*. (1911). Drypoint, 9¹/₁₆ x 7³/₁₆″. Signed lower right in pencil. (Sch. R 165, III/III). The Museum of Modern Art, New York. Purchase. Ill. p. 53

170. *Rich Farmers (Grossbauern)*. (1918). Etching and aquatint, 8¹⁵/₁₆ x 11¹⁵/₁₆″. Signed lower right in pencil. (Sch. R 193 IV/IV). The Museum of Modern Art, New York. Gift of Mrs. John D. Rockefeller, Jr.

171. *Slaves (Sklaven)*. (1918). Etching and aquatint, 12³/₈ x 8″. Signed lower right in pencil. (Sch. R 198). The Museum of Modern Art, New York. Gift of Mrs. John D. Rockefeller, Jr.

172. *The Animal Lover (Der Tierfreund)*. (1918). Etching and aquatint, 11¹³/₁₆ x 8¹¹/₁₆″. Signed lower right in pencil. (Sch. R 203, II/II). The Museum of Modern Art, New York. Gift of Mrs. John D. Rockefeller, Jr.

173. *The Esthete (Der Aesthete)*. (1918). Etching and aquatint, 12 x 9¹/₂″. Signed lower right in pencil. (Sch. R 205). Nolde Foundation, Seebüll

* 174. *Flood (Überschwemmung)*. (1922). Etching, 9⁷/₈ x 16¹⁵/₁₆″. (Sch. R 223, III). Nolde Foundation, Seebüll. Ill. p. 54

175. *Sailboat (Segelboot)*. (1922). Etching, 16³/₄ x 9⁷/₈″. Signed lower right in pencil. (Sch. R 227). Nolde Foundation, Seebüll

WOODCUTS

* 176. *The Large Bird (Der Grosse Vogel)*. (1906). Woodcut, 6¹/₂ x 8⁵/₁₆″. Signed lower right in pencil. (Sch. H 9, III). Nolde Foundation, Seebüll. Ill. p. 56

177. *The Italian (Italiener)*. (1906). Woodcut, 11³/₈ x 9¹/₁₆″. Signed lower right in pencil. (Sch. H 26). Nolde Foundation, Seebüll

* 178. *Fishing Boat (Fischdampfer)*. (1910). Woodcut, 12 x 15³/₄″. Signed lower right in pencil. (Sch. H 34). Nolde Foundation, Seebüll. Ill. p. 56

* 179. *Prophet*. (1912). Woodcut, 12⁵/₈ x 8³/₄″. Signed lower right in pencil. (Sch. H 110). The Museum of Modern Art, New York. Given Anonymously. Ill. p. 57

180. *Woman's Head, III (Frauenkopf, III)*. (1912). Woodcut, 11⁷/₈ x 8¹³/₁₆″. Signed lower right in pencil. (Sch. H 116, III). The Museum of Modern Art, New York. Gift of Mrs. John D. Rockefeller, Jr.

181. *Serf (Knecht)*. (1912). Woodcut, 11¹³/₁₆ x 9¹/₂″. Signed lower right in pencil. (Sch. H 117, III). Nolde Foundation, Seebüll

182. *Candle Dancers (Kerzentänzerinnen)*. (1917). Woodcut, 12 x 9¹/₄″. Signed lower right in pencil. (Sch. H 127, V(?)/V). The Museum of Modern Art, New York. Larry Aldrich Fund

* 183. *Family (Familie)*. (1917). Woodcut, 9⁷/₁₆ x 12⁵/₈″. Signed lower right in pencil. (Sch. H 128, II). Nolde Foundation, Seebüll. Ill. p. 57

184. *Young Couple (Junges Paar)*. (1917). Woodcut, 12⁵/₈ x 9¹/₁₆″. Signed lower right in pencil. (Sch. H 133, III/III). The Museum of Modern Art, New York. Purchase

185. *The Doctors (Doktoren)*. (1922). Woodcut, 19⁷/₈ x 27¹³/₁₆″, Signed lower right in pencil. (Sch. H 166, II/III). The Museum of Modern Art, New York. Gift of Mrs. John D. Rockefeller, Jr.

186. *Self Portrait with Pipe (Kopf mit Pfeife).* (1907). Lithograph, 15³/₄ x 11¹/₈″. Signed lower right in pencil. (Sch. L 5, b/b). The Museum of Modern Art, New York. Gift of Mr. and Mrs. Carroll Cartwright

187. *Alice.* 1907. Lithograph, printed in color, 13¹/₄ x 8⁹/₁₆″. Signed lower right in pencil. (Sch. L 7 a/b). The Museum of Modern Art, New York. Curt Valentin Bequest

188. *Alice.* 1907. Lithograph, printed in black, 13¹/₈ x 8¹/₂″. Not signed. (Sch. L 7, b/b). The Museum of Modern Art, New York. Purchase

189. *Sonderburg (Bei Sonderburg).* (1907). Lithograph, printed in color, 12¹/₈ x 19³/₄″. Signed lower right in pencil. (Sch. L. 19, final proof). The Museum of Modern Art, New York. Gift of Mr. and Mrs. Eugene Victor Thaw

190. *Bright Day (Heller Tag).* (1907). Lithograph, 11 x 19¹/₁₆″. (Sch. L 20). Nolde Foundation, Seebüll

191. *Tingel Tangel, II.* 1907. Lithograph, 12³/₄ x 18⁷/₈″. Signed lower right in pencil. (Sch. L 26). The Museum of Modern Art, New York. Purchase

192. *Man in a Top Hat (Mann in Zylinder).* (1911). Lithograph, printed in brown-black, 23³/₈ x 17¹/₂″. Signed lower right in pencil. (Sch. L 39, IIb). The Museum of Modern Art, New York. Gift of Mrs. Donald B. Straus

193. *Profile.* (1911). Lithograph, 6¹/₁₆ x 3⁷/₁₆″. Signed lower right in pencil. (Sch. L 44 (?)). The Museum of Modern Art, New York. Purchase

194. *Young Woman in Hat (Junge Frau in Hut).* (1911). Lithograph, 6¹⁵/₁₆ x 3³/₄″. Signed lower right in pencil. (Sch. L 45). The Museum of Modern Art, New York. Purchase

195. *The Three Kings (Die Heiligen Drei Könige).* (1913). Lithograph, printed in color, 25¹/₄ x 21″. Not signed. (Sch. L 49 2 Or 5F). The Museum of Modern Art, New York. Purchase

196. *The Peddler (Händler).* (1913). Lithograph, printed in color, 24¹/₂ x 15⁷¹/₁₆″. Signed lower right in pencil. (Sch. L 50). The Minneapolis Institute of Arts, Miscellaneous. Purchase Funds

197. *Discussion (Diskussion).* (1913). Lithograph, printed in color, from three stones, 29⁷/₁₆ x 23¹/₄″. Signed lower right in pencil. (Sch. L 51, C2/2). The Museum of Modern Art, New York. Purchase

198. *Young Couple (Das junge Paar).* (1913). Lithograph, printed in color from three stones, 24¹/₂ x 20¹/₁₆″. Signed lower right in pencil. (Sch. L 52 CI/E, eleventh variation). The Museum of Modern Art, New York. Mrs. John D. Rockefeller, Jr. Purchase Fund

* 199. *Young Couple (Das junge Paar).* (1913). Lithograph, printed in color from three stones, 24⁷/₁₆ x 20¹/₁₆″. Signed lower right in pencil. (Sch. L 52, DII/E, sixth variation). The Museum of Modern Art, New York. Mrs. John D. Rockefeller, Jr. Purchase Fund. Ill. p. 58

200. *Young Couple (Das junge Paar).* (1913). Lithograph, printed in color from four stones, 24¹/₂ x 20⁵/₁₆″. Signed lower right in pencil. (Sch. L 52, D/E). The Museum of Modern Art, New York. Gift of Mrs. John D. Rockefeller, Jr.

201. *Mother and Child (Mutter und Kind).* (1913). Lithograph, printed in color from two stones, 18⁷/₈ x 17¹/₈″. Signed lower right in pencil. (Sch. L 53). Nolde Foundation, Seebüll

202. *Grotesques (Grotesken).* (1913). Lithograph, printed in color from four stones, 23 x 19¹/₄″. Signed lower right in pencil. (Sch. L 54, D/E). The Museum of Modern Art, New York. Purchase

* 203. *Dancer (Tänzerin),* 1913. Lithograph, printed in color, 21¹/₁₀ x 27¹/₈″. Signed lower right in pencil. (Sch. L 56). Collection Mrs. Gertrud A. Mellon, New York

204. *Windmill (Windmühle).* (1913). Lithograph, printed in color, 22⁷/₁₆ x 27³/₄″. (Sch. L 61, D 1). Nolde Foundation, Seebüll

205. *Fall Landscape.* (1926). Lithograph, printed in color, 23¹/₄ x 31¹/₄″. (Not in Sch.). Nolde Foundation, Seebüll

206. *Windmill on the Shore.* (1926). Lithograph, printed in color, 23¹/₄ x 31¹/₄″. Signed lower right in pencil. (Not in Sch.). The Museum of Modern Art, New York. James Thrall Soby Fund

207. *The Sea (Meer).* (c. 1926). Lithograph, printed in color, 23³/₄ x 31³/₈″. Signed lower right in pencil. (Not in Sch.). Collection Mrs. Heinz Schultz, Great Neck, New York

Dates enclosed in parantheses do not appear on the paintings. In dimensions height precedes width. Works marked with an asterisk are illustrated. The German titles for the oils are generally those Nolde himself gave to his canvases; those for the prints are given by Schiefler (bibl. 21, 22). Watercolors and drawings, rarely titled by Nolde himself, are listed with the English form of the titles indicated by the respective lenders. We are indebted to Werner Haftmann for supplying titles for the "Unpainted Pictures".

SELECTIVE INDEX

figures in italics are illustrations